of Its Own

NUTLEY VELO

Old Fashion
Candy
FRESH SQUEEZED

PIZZALAND

PIZZALAND

TASTEE SUB SHOP

OPEN DAILY FAM. 11 AM

EXIT 145

The Oranges

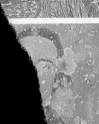

W. W.

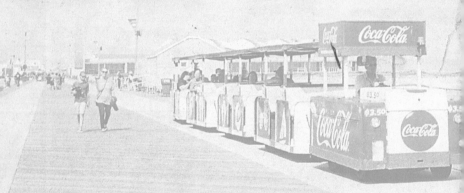

NEW J

Rutgers University Press

New Brunswick, Camden, and
Newark, New Jersey, and London

ERSEY

FAN CLUB

Artists and
Writers Celebrate
the Garden State

Edited by
Kerri Sullivan

Library of Congress Cataloging-in-Publication Data

Names: Sullivan, Kerri, editor.

Title: New Jersey fan club : 40 voices celebrate the Garden State / edited by Kerri Sullivan.

Description: New Brunswick : Rutgers University Press, [2022] | "An anthology about New Jersey from the creator of Jersey Collective." | Includes bibliographical references.

Identifiers: LCCN 2021039567 | ISBN 9781978825604 (paperback) | ISBN 9781978825611 (hardback) | ISBN 9781978825628 (epub) | ISBN 9781978825635 (mobi) | ISBN 9781978825642 (pdf)

Subjects: LCSH: New Jersey—History, Local—Anecdotes. | New Jersey—Social life and customs—Anecdotes. | New Jersey—Biography—Anecdotes.

Classification: LCC F134.6 .N55 2022 | DDC 974.9—dc23/eng/20220118

LC record available at https://lccn.loc.gov/2021039567

A British Cataloging-in-Publication record for this book is available from the British Library.

This collection copyright © 2022 by Rutgers, The State University of New Jersey

Individual chapters copyright © 2022 in the names of their authors

All rights reserved

No part of this book may be reproduced or utilized in any form or by any means, electronic or mechanical, or by any information storage and retrieval system, without written permission from the publisher. Please contact Rutgers University Press, 106 Somerset Street, New Brunswick, NJ 08901. The only exception to this prohibition is "fair use" as defined by U.S. copyright law.

References to internet websites (URLs) were accurate at the time of writing. Neither the author nor Rutgers University Press is responsible for URLs that may have expired or changed since the manuscript was prepared.

∞ The paper used in this publication meets the requirements of the American National Standard for Information Sciences—Permanence of Paper for Printed Library Materials, ANSI Z39.48-1992.

www.rutgersuniversitypress.org

Manufactured in the United States of America

For Mom and Susan, for everything

CONTENTS

NEW JERSEY FAN CLUB

Illustration by Alex Flannery

Introduction

KERRI SULLIVAN

I would have no trouble writing an entire book about New Jersey.

I would tell you that I've lived in five counties and was born in a sixth. I've lived half a mile from a military fort. I've lived four blocks from the ocean. I've lived in flight paths and along train lines. I've lived adjacent to the Great Swamp. I've lived on a street where, if I walked to the top of its hill, I could see a sliver of the New York City skyline. I've lived on land that was once beside a horse farm. At various points in my life, I've laid in bed and listened to crickets, trains, foxes, church bells, seagulls, and bugles playing "Taps." All of this in the same state, no place farther than an hour from the next.

I would calculate, somehow, the number of hours I've driven on my state's highways and tell you which stretches of the Parkway feel like home. I'd share realizations I've had while stuck in traffic on 287. I'd tell you that the first time I ever drove a car, my driving instructor directed me to Route 18, around traffic circles, over the newly built Route 35 bridge in Belmar, along the ocean, and to a Wawa, where she bought soup that she ate in the car as I drove.

I would tell you about the diners where I formed bonds with friends over plates of cheese fries, where I drank milkshakes at arguably inappropriate hours. How it always felt normal to me to be able to procure excellent take-out from almost every cuisine on Earth without having to drive very far. How I didn't realize there was anything special about the pizza or bagels I grew up eating until I traveled to beautiful places where I was served terrible pizza by people who looked at me funny when I tried to order a "plain pie."

I would tell you that my great-grandmother packed cookies for Nabisco and my grandmother worked in Jersey City for the Erie Railroad and my mother went to college across the country, where no one who asked her what kind of music she liked had ever heard of Bruce Springsteen (yet).

I would tell you I remember a history unit in elementary school focused on our state, culminating with a trip to the State House in Trenton, where I was captivated by a carpet depicting some of our state symbols—violets, goldfinches, oak leaves. Back at school, I remember a party where our parents were somehow roped into baking cakes shaped vaguely like each county, which were frosted with different colors and assembled together on tables in our gymnasium, a red icing star drawn over our town.

I would show you photographs from when I worked as a historical interpreter at Allaire Village and Longstreet Farm, where I dressed in historically accurate clothing and felt connected to the past. I would tell you how when I interned in the city, at the Met, I commuted four hours a day on a combination of NJ Transit trains, buses, and subways. How I got to know the rhythm of that train so well that I knew when it would come to a quiet hum as it drifted across bridges, knew when the lights were about to go off. How at first I was bewildered by all of the frantic New Jerseyans dressed in business casual attire who ran through Penn Station, but by the end of my internship, I realized I'd become one of them.

I would analyze the perceptions other people have of my home state that have always confounded me. As a teenager, I pored over issues of *Weird NJ*, wondering if other places also had entire magazines dedicated to their strangeness. In college, across the river in Philadelphia, I met people from all over the country (and world) who had one of two reactions when I told them where I was from: "I wouldn't have guessed that" or "That makes sense." I was never sure if I reflected or subverted my home state. I was less sure what it was about me that either gave me away or incited doubt. Whenever anyone said "I'm sorry" or "Ew" when I said where I was from, I sat with their assertion not only that New Jersey was an oil-tank-ridden, smelly, overcrowded shithole but also, naturally, that I was supposed to agree with them.

If I was writing a book about New Jersey, I would tell you that Sandy Hook is the place I most want to go after something bad happens to me. There's something restorative about not only the salt air but also the place itself. It feels wild, ever-changing; it's damaged but resilient. It's weathered wars and hurricanes and the threat of development, and it's still there.

I would tell you I once knew a relationship was over as we spent the day in Princeton, the state's top-rated sorbet tasteless on my tongue. That my family's car was once stolen from the Willowbrook Mall parking lot while we were at the movies. That as a teenager I didn't go to the mall as often as I did downtown Red Bank and that almost every place I frequented has now been turned into something else. That when I walk around Bradley Beach and Ocean Grove, I gawk at the houses and wonder if I could ever afford even the shittiest one.

I would tell you what New Jersey has given me, and I would tell you what it has taken. I would tell you what New Jersey made me, and I would tell you why it matters.

But I wasn't interested in making that book. I was much more interested in what other people had to say.

This book grew out of a project I created called Jersey Collective, a collaborative Instagram account that a different person takes over each week. Every day since the project began in March 2014, contributors have shared at least one photo taken in New Jersey. The result is a space that celebrates our state's natural, cultural, and historical treasures through the eyes of an ever-changing group of residents and transplants. Hundreds of people from a variety of backgrounds have participated over the years. Each week brings a new perspective and creates new connections. The project quickly grew into a community that extended beyond Instagram to include photography shows, meet-ups, and other events, as well as collaborations with other arts and culture organizations.

Jersey Collective showed me, and our tens of thousands of followers, that New Jersey has a lot to offer and a lot to look at—and that it doesn't look the same to everyone. Someone from Salem County experiences Jersey differently from someone in Hudson County. We have something in common, a shared claim to the same state, but every one of us sees this place through our own eyes, through the lenses of our own experiences, from our own particular piece of land.

One of my goals as an editor was to make a book that does the same thing as Jersey Collective: brings together the voices of many people and gives them a space to share what New Jersey looks like through their eyes as well as how it's shaped them.

I could've made infinite versions of this book, choosing to focus on different subjects and places, but it would be impossible to include everything. New Jersey is a wildly diverse place across every metric, from our landscapes to the people who call it home. Everyone's experiences within the same place can vary wildly but still be true. There is no singular New Jersey experience. That's why we argue over whether Central Jersey exists (it does) and over whether it's called "Pork Roll" or "Taylor Ham" (I'm staying out of that one). I'm interested in the universality *and* the things that make us different.

I hope the choices I have made resonate. I hope it makes you feel proud of your state and helps you see it in a new way. I hope you'll say, "I didn't know that," and then, on another page, "I feel that."

This book is not meant to be a travel guide. You won't find any lists of the state's top breweries or best small towns here. Still, you'll be inspired to look at New Jersey in a different way, to look closer at the historical markers in your hometown, and to explore things the state has to offer that you may not have noticed before. The work in this book includes personal essays on a wide range of subjects, researched essays on historical topics, comics, interviews, and other surprises. Not only will you learn interesting facts about our state, but you'll meet some people for whom being from (or having experienced) New Jersey is a crucial part of their identities and has helped shape them as people and artists.

I hope you, no matter your experience with New Jersey, find something in this book that feels true to you.

Illustration by Haley Simone

Why Do They Hate Us?

MATTHEW TAUB

During my junior year of high school, I mounted a longshot campaign for student body president. As a Jersey kid who commuted to a New York City school, my strategy was never in doubt: I would roast my home state—viciously, repeatedly—and appeal to my classmates' disdain for it. I joked that the internet hadn't made it to the state yet, that I rode to school via horseback, that I communicated with neighbors via smoke signals. This seemed more promising than campaigning on substance; six years of commuting had taught me how to speak another state's language.

Everyone from Jersey knows the score. We are constantly confronted, from all sides, by accusations of inferiority, provincialism, even repulsiveness. George Carlin quipped that we should be called the "Tollbooth State" instead of the "Garden State"; in *Sleeper*, Woody Allen observed that intelligent life is present everywhere in the universe . . . except for parts of one state. A more recent barb, in Lin-Manuel Miranda's *Hamilton*, weaves these assumptions into the story of the nation's founding, explaining that duels had to go down in Jersey because "everything is legal" here. These are jokes, of course, and funny ones. Less amusing is a

2015 YouGov survey, which found that New Jersey is both the least liked state in the United States *and* the *only* state with a net-negative approval rating (−10!).

My speech got a lot of laughs, but I suppose it's only fitting that I lost the school election. Winning would have severely complicated my narrative.

With full understanding that the stakes are ultimately low—that Jerseyphobia is not a dangerous prejudice, that parts of the state are in fact enormously wealthy and home to the most privileged—I wanted to find out why: *Why* is the Jersey joke universal shorthand? How did we accrue stereotypes recognized around the world? Other regions of the country, like the South, certainly take some collective shit from outsiders, but no single state gets it like New Jersey. (*Why?* These hecklers have clearly never been to Florida.)

I reached out to three experts on the state to advise my inquiry. The first, Michael Aaron Rockland, is a cultural historian of New Jersey at Rutgers University who has written four books about the state. Second was Kevin Coyne, a journalist who covered New Jersey for years at the *New York Times* and who serves as the official historian for Freehold—the hometown he shares with Bruce Springsteen. (Coyne was also my advisor at Columbia Journalism School.) Finally, I spoke with Jack Antonoff, the Grammy-winning leader of the band Bleachers and a songwriter and record producer who has collaborated with Taylor Swift, Lorde, and Bruce Springsteen, to name just a few. Our families have been summertime neighbors on the Jersey Shore since before I was born.

These men all come from different generations and from different parts of the state. And yet they agree, in general, that our infamy is driven by New Yorkers (e.g., Carlin, Allen, Miranda). To people from the big city—and, mind you, it is *the* big city—everything beyond its limits is "flyover country," Rockland explains. And because Jersey is just over the bridge, it in particular is "the beginning of no man's land," distinguished only as the gateway to nowhere. Coyne agrees that New Yorkers look down on us because we're not them but suggests that others resent our *connections* to the city, taking us for lower-rent versions of obnoxious Manhattanites—just as rude with none of the ritz. For Antonoff, New Jersey is simply overshadowed by the monster across the river, forever Scottie Pippen to next door's Michael Jordan. We are "the little brother of little brothers," he says, cursed by sheer proximity. It was written, from the start, into our very names: York, an ancient, walled British city founded by the Romans; Jersey, a tiny "Crown dependency" floating in the English Channel. Raise your hand if you've ever said you're from "the greater New York area."

Antonoff's observation is obvious enough but has compounding implications. The dynamic between New York and New Jersey, he says, is "quite literally medieval," with a small body of water cordoning the castle off from the commoners (many of whom commute to keep the castle running, but that's another essay). This puts New Jersey in a completely unique situation, he says. While other great urban centers sprawl out gradually into appendant neighborhoods—think Berlin, London, Los Angeles, Tokyo—there is a fixed point at which New York's energy stops and New Jersey's begins. This makes all eighty-seven hundred square miles of New Jersey synonymous with "not–New York." A place that's not just lesser but homogeneous: one turnpike-length basket of disposables.

The irony is that few places come close to New Jersey in complexity and diversity. Ours is the most densely populated state—we're even more densely packed than India, Rockland points out. Approximately 15 percent of the state's population is Black, and immigrants from over one hundred countries number in the millions (and over one million more New Jersey-ans are children of immigrants). Coyne recalls the nine-year "interregnum" he spent in Massachusetts, his wife's home state. "I hated, hated, hated" it, says the fifth-generation Freehold native. "It was so fucking white." Our landscapes may be as diverse as our people. "Take this from someone who's toured the country for their entire life," says Antonoff. Turning just a few miles in New Jersey, you'll run into "beaches, mountains, farms, cities." People laugh when he says so, but it reminds him of "a mini version of Europe," where one cultural zone instantly becomes another. Maybe this explains why, in Rockland's experience, foreigners are quicker to recognize and admire our state's "energy." It's no wonder that New Jersey, in its dynamism, has birthed so many famous progeny: from Meryl Streep to Lauryn Hill to Count Basie, the list is astonishingly long.

And yet we're seen as "America's armpit": the state that exists, as one high school classmate told me, to serve as "a bridge between New York City and Philadelphia," cheap gas available along the way. Coyne recalls the condescension of his neighbors in Massachusetts, who saw New Jersey as a place with "no history." Never mind that more than two hundred locations throughout the state bear Native American place-names or that this was the first state to ratify the entire Bill of Rights or that the Battle of Monmouth was the largest land battle of the American Revolution—never mind that as Washington crossed the "Delaware," he was heading to freaking *Trenton*. "You had a little skirmish up here," Coyne thought to himself in Massachusetts. "We did all the fucking war down here in New Jersey." It's worth noting—again, with full awareness that only pride is at stake—how reflective this is of other, far-more-nefarious bigotries: the idea of a people without a past, who don't author culture but who need it supplied by others. It's as if the state bubbled up sometime in the twentieth century, fully formed in concrete, populated by proto-Snookis and Tony Sopranos. Being so maligned, New Jerseyans have been known to respond by rallying together and taking vocal pride in their shared identity. As usual, outsiders find a way to hate that, too.

I sometimes even wonder if Springsteen's status as Jersey's great beloved ambassador has a way of working against us. "Bruce did more for this state's image than anyone, I think, in history," says Rockland, and I actually doubt that any other American figure has ever been so closely associated with a single state. You can be traveling on another continent, say you're from New Jersey, and reasonably expect to get "BRUUUUCE"-d in response. We are rightly proud. The trouble is that those who don't revere him *patronize* him, even if they do so unknowingly. Indeed, there are Bruce fans who see him as quaint, quirky, a bit of a yokel—a Shore rat with a funny accent, rambling about cars and girls. Has he influenced their image of New Jersey, then, or have Jersey stereotypes influenced their image of *him*? I fear that Bruce (whom I worship) is sometimes used to reinforce a reputation that precedes him, for he satisfies his state's archetype better than, say, Meryl—the image of elegance. Bruce can give those who look for it the New Jersey they want. Of course, he does capture some fundamental things about this place: the scrappiness, the highways, the city skyline in the distance. The point is that no one person should stand in for eight million; neither he nor we deserve to be so simplified.

Since 2015, Antonoff has hosted an annual music festival, "Shadow of the City," at the famed Stone Pony in Bruce's own Asbury Park. It's just one of the many ways in which he consciously, intentionally, pushes New Jersey to the forefront of his music and persona. Some of that, inescapably, is a tribute to Springsteen. It also draws interest from those who enjoy the Jersey brand, however ironically—a nostalgic little world of boardwalks and affable toughs. Mainly, though, Antonoff just wants to bring his audience closer to the place as it really is. It's almost paradoxical, but he believes that Jersey music sounds bigger and wider than New York City music: think Clarence Clemons's immense saxophone versus The Strokes' wiry guitars, Whitney Houston's belting versus Lou Reed's spoken word. That all speaks to our "desperate attempt to describe this place," he says, a battle we're always engaged in. There's "no need to describe New York City" or any place that's treated with the proper respect.

And so we'll continue to try, whether or not anyone wants to hear it. "I'm always learning shit" about this place, Coyne says with a proud chuckle. At one point, he gets up to close his office door as his wife walks by and asks, "Are you talking about fucking New Jersey again?"

The Challenge

FRANKIE HUANG

I Pledge Allegiance to the Mall

ERINN SALGE

Like many young New Jerseyans, being trusted to spend a Friday night alone at the mall was a rite of passage. Being dropped off by the van-load in the parking lot of the Rainforest Café (but never actually eating there) felt somehow bigger, more portentous than "going downtown." Our families went downtown, but the mall was more alluring, promising kids from different towns, the movie theater, the food court. In my youth, the mall was Menlo, anchored by Nordstrom and Macy's, and when the Barnes and Noble moved in during my teenage years, it was like anything you could want was there. I'm a bit younger than the true mall heyday of the 1980s, my own teen years marked by 9/11, pop punk on the radio, and the doomed low-rise jeans trend. But it still held its allure, even as I couldn't afford anything at Abercrombie or Bebe, where everyone cooler and richer than me seemed to shop.

When I moved to suburban Atlanta for an AmeriCorps term after four New Jersey college years, I was alone in the world, with no other family members for thousands of miles. I lived on a campsite without running water, surrounded by crunchier people who were enlivened by fresh air and the sound of coyotes yelling at night. I stood out as a northerner, an introvert—someone who felt perpetually out of place, even in a life I'd wholeheartedly chosen. During my first weeks there, I navigated to the edge of town, to the comforts of a known quantity in a life where I was continually solving for x: the mall. I wandered the wide-open spaces, marveling at the differences between New Jersey and Georgia (the indignity of sales tax on clothing!), but mostly found a sort of calm in the sameness. I bit into an Auntie Anne's, the butter leaching through the paper, and thought of the worksheets I gave to my students, incomprehensible to them and exasperating to me. Life felt hard, but everything from the soft lighting to the soft rock felt easy at the mall. I experienced unrivaled Zen as I brushed my fingertips over the displays at Piercing Pagoda. Maybe it was the walking that healed my head, or maybe the air-conditioned corridors of the Arbor Place Mall was the one place I could go that felt more like home, where I was New Jersey Erinn again. If I squinted my eyes, I could imagine I was home, minutes away from a hot shower and everyone who loved me.

After my AmeriCorps term, I moved back to New Jersey, where the comforts of suburbia greeted me with open arms after a year surrounded by trees and nature that had a tendency to find its way inside my cabin, even with a locked door. I was so Jersey that I decided to only apply to Rutgers for grad school, and mercifully I got in. As I built my career and went to school simultaneously, I spent Friday afternoons back at Menlo Mall, still mostly just perusing. Other people had nature. I had the food court.

Something about the monotony of walking, feeling the synthetic fabrics at The Limited, and the promise of an adult career and its spending money lent the air a frisson of hope. In high school, the mall was about who you meant to see. In adulthood, I kept my eyes down, begging the universe not to let me run into anyone from adolescence and have to talk about living at home. I bought fountain Diet Cokes and let my brain detach a bit, the stresses of working and going to school oozing out as I padded around the route from Macy's to Nordstrom, rarely stopping to buy a thing.

Time marched on, stores closed, others opened. I sought refuge from Superstorm Sandy at the Champps in the mall and applied eyeliner in the darkened parking lot while my power was out. With a proposal and a new job came another personality adjustment: I left Central New Jersey, its Menlo (and lesser Woodbridge), and went north—specifically, to a home in Livingston, midway between its eponymous mall and the ritzier Short Hills.

The latter of which I will adopt. Not right away, of course. Our first years are leaner as my husband and I adjust to our new lives together. I rushed home from work to feed our dog, who aged along with us and our house. The mall mostly felt too fancy and home too inviting. I realized I didn't need to escape, and I embraced the feeling of burrowing in, enjoying long winter nights on our impossibly comfy couch and sunny summer days on our deck.

And then years later, the baby comes and, with him, a squirrely need deep inside to just get out and leave some days. He is a spring baby, and for every walk we take around the South Mountain Reservoir, I find myself driving down JFK Parkway too—back to the mall. When we go for the first time, he's maybe too young, small enough that the cashier at Starbucks squints at me and asks, "How *old* is that baby?" Becoming a mother feels right, essential to me, and yet the change sends my anxious brain seeking comfort, and where else does one find it in New Jersey but at the mall?

For the first months, nothing I try on fits, but the mall gives me somewhere to be. I eventually pick up some pumping-friendly blazers and blouses at Banana Republic, a promise that someday I'll go back to work, at a new job, and balance the life of mom and librarian. I shimmy the stroller through the narrow clearance aisles of Anthropologie, imagining the person I'm becoming draped in shawls, lighting fancy candles. I'm a Short Hills person now, the low lighting soothing the sleeping baby, the promise of the higher-end shops meaning better things to come. I still mostly browse. It's like it's permanently etched in my brain that malls are for walking and looking and being, not really for making purchases. But when summer ends and I go back to work, I still take the baby and his stroller to the mall on weekends, rebooting my mind after the week's complicated balancing act of parenting and working.

And then a change: we move to a new house, in the midst of a pandemic. I prepare mentally to leave Short Hills geography and enter Rockaway instead, the final stop in my life's game board of Mall Madness. With all the malls closed, I can't soothe myself with retail in the midst of a national catastrophe. I long to wander through the lavender-scented air of Lush and the bright lights of Sephora, thinking of how the casual smelling and sampling days are over. I drive past the mall, hulking and empty, on rides to get my now-toddler to nap.

Out of necessity, I found myself walking with my son in downtown Denville instead. And as I watch my son eagerly point out the ice cream on the Denville Dairy sign, wave to the gaggle of old men who camp outside Smart World Coffee, and race to the ad hoc Marian grotto behind Faith and Begorrah, I wonder if time has come full circle and my years at the mall are coming to an end. I was raised with the cozy downtown charm of Metuchen. I remember rec-soccer pizza parties at Roberto's, marathon gossip sessions at Brewed Awakenings, and the summer programs at the library. Small-town life, unavailable to me in Georgia, in Livingston, and when I was trying to avoid old classmates in Metuchen, is suddenly within my grasp again. Nature has its charms as we hunt for frogs in Morristown, but it's on the tidy sidewalks and broad intersections that I feel myself relax.

The mall allows for versions of ourselves: in mirrors, in sales clerks knocking on the door, in our inner monologues, and in the Muzak turned up loud. I tried to find myself as a teenager pawing through the crates at CD World and again as a young professional sliding into cocktail dresses for wedding after wedding after wedding. Downtown is where I simply am, fully realized, a contented working parent. My reflection in the windows of the mom-and-pop stores looks different, more self-assured, than the one in the dressing rooms of J. Crew. And so we walk up and down Broad Street as I imagine the new life I've stepped into: one where maybe I don't have the need to escape to the mall but instead find release and comfort and clarity in the little shop windows, the ornate architecture of Hunan Taste begging to be touched by little hands, the charm of seeing the same gaggles of people every morning.

The mall is aspiring, becoming, trying desperately to be at peace, and the crosswalks and diners are where I can simply be. Maybe for this next phase of life, I don't need a mall. Maybe downtown will do.

Suburban South Jersey

LAUREN H. ADAMS

"Suburban South Jersey" is an ongoing series that began in 2014. This body of work examines the vernacular landscape of southern New Jersey from the perspectives of both a resident and an outsider in one. The most noticeable recurrence in this series is the presence of discarded furniture, largely sofas. The sofas reveal to the viewer a glimpse into the lifestyle of these former owners—personality, style, financial status. They also serve as evidence of the existence of residents of South Jersey, who themselves are absent from the imagery. The photographs in this selection were largely captured in townships of Burlington County such as South-ampton, Medford, Marlton, and Mount Laurel.

Selling Balloons to New Jersey

BRANDON HARRISON

When I think of Atlantic City, before I think of Monopoly or cheap seafood buffets, I think of the warm slosh of seagull poop on the side of my face.

As soon as the bitterness of the Northeast cold subsided and out-door events ramped up, my father, Al, would load his Econoline 250 with balloons, silly string, and novelties of all sorts. We'd ride from festival to festival, working sixteen-hour days, from setup to breakdown, standing all day in the sun until nightfall. Carnival people are pejoratively known as "carnies," people who travel from place to place running rickety rides and scamming people with rigged games. We definitely weren't that. But it's a workplace analogue I find apt. I like to say we were "festies."

This enterprising festival lifestyle gestated in Newark, within a close-knit family. My grandmother Clementina came to America from Trinidad as a young woman and had six children, fourteen grandchildren, and more greats and great-greats than I can count. Among these children, they managed to have a small business, an industry, that they could share in.

Whether or not every family member wanted to participate or deemed the work undignified, we've all participated in some way or fashion. Every cousin, child, niece, or nephew has had a day out with Uncle Al or Uncle Tristan. Considering their formative years witnessing domestic abuse, losing a home to a devastating fire, and having a grandfather brutally slain by the police during the Newark riots, this quirky little business is a hallmark of resilience—so much so that the details of these generational scars were only revealed to me at thirty years old. Family is interesting in that way. You never totally know the depth of the experience of people who supposedly you share the most intimate connection with.

What we actually did was always hard to describe to other people, but it was essentially vending at parades, festivals, and large gatherings across the entirety of New Jersey and the eastern seaboard. Al was brought into the world of event sales as a kid in Newark in the 1970s. His mentor, Mr. Ulysses Richardson, was a Newark businessman who had concessions and merchandise contracts with a number of venues. My dad started as a "car boy" who watched Uly's double-parked car when he bought inventory in New York. Eventually, as a teen, he was able to sell merchandise when shows came through Newark's Symphony Hall. On his first big trip away from home, Al had the pleasure of selling light-up hats at a Sylvester concert at the Fountain Casino in Aberdeen. Some kid named Michael Bivins, from an opening act called New Edition, harassed him for one of those cool hats to wear.

Al wanted to set out on his own, so he picked up an old merchandise trick from Mr. Richardson's crew. Drop a sprinkle of uncooked grits, rice, or oats into colorful balloons, inflate, and tie with a rubber band: Boom.

A noise-making punch balloon. During the early 1980s, a summer after-noon in the park was entertainment du jour for the people of Newark, so Al set out into the parks and block parties of the city with these sim-ple balloons and made a nice bit of disposable income for an industrious college student.

As Al was the youngest boy in a family of six, this little business was mostly a silly curiosity for the rest of the family. Just another member of the family trying to find a way to make some extra change, as they had done since their days running a family candy stand from Grandma's excess inventory of Smarties from her job at the CeDe Candy Factory. However, Al's eldest brother, Tristan, got a bit more than curious. The way my uncle describes it, he "scoffed" at his brother walking the streets selling mer-chandise. Nevertheless, Al invited him to the park one afternoon; he took off from his insurance job, shook off a bit of condescension, and made the easiest thousand bucks of his life, one balloon at a time.

From there, the business grew, from summer days in the Weequa-hic Park to vendor licenses and scouring newspaper ads for public events across the state. Al never liked people calling it "a good hustle" because of the negative connotation. He always likened the roving, barker-style work to providing good customer service. His mentality changed a business that sold generic patterned balloons into one that sold branded Nickel-odeon and Disney inflates, plus colorful bottles of sand art, and supported entire families. While Al and Tristan were its core, an ever-changing cast of nieces, nephews, sons, daughters, cousins, husbands, wives, and even grandmothers found themselves tending a booth or pushing a cart of balloons. As one of those sons, I feel these languid summer days past preserved in amber, but the specifics of the family's collective memory reveal an experience broader than just my own.

Uncle Tristan doesn't remember the seagull poop, but he does remember the name of that particular festival, even after vending at hundreds of others. That poop graced my cheek at the 1996 Kentucky Avenue Renaissance Festival. He also remembers we made a good amount of money that day. He remembers when my cousin Star warded off some enterprising little people with sticky fingers reaching toward his table through a wire fence at a busy festival.

Al remembers after the first day at Kentucky Avenue, a storm hit the shore and blew our canopy tent—that we thought we'd tied down—a few hundreds yards down the road. He remembers having a huge day capitalizing on the Pokémon card craze in 1998 and getting spooked when rumors of counterfeit wholesalers came to light.

My little sister Alana recalls sleeping head to toe with my brother Allen on a jerry-rigged bed in the back of the van when Dad drove home late after a festival. She remembers working a day with my Uncle Tristan and how it was "lit" to get $75. She remembers working a ten-hour event in an underground concourse with, *gasp*, no cellphone service.

This nostalgia doesn't mean that things were always fanciful. Sometimes, I'll fondly remember working the booth at Newark's Bergen Street at an age as young as eight, somehow managing to stay safe with hundreds of dollars in my pocket. My brother vividly recalls being that age and getting robbed for his inventory of light-up toys in that exact same city. Stories of theft, robbery, disputes, and aggressive swindlers abound, but nevertheless, this business has persevered.

The Fourth of July is always the most successful day of the summer season. The nearly weeklong series of festivals and firework displays allowed us to bounce to anywhere that had a display that day, from Newark to Neptune. We've done cultural festivals, Pride, St. Patrick's Day, and Puerto Rican parades. But the Fourth brought everyone out, and they all wanted light-up toys. Glow sticks two for a dollar. Light-up swords for five bucks. Colorful headbands, flashing pacifiers, necklaces, wands, and balls. Harmless bang-snap fireworks that kids love. The energy of those nights etched them permanently in my mind, but now they feel even more important as a symbol.

The last time I vended, my father, younger sister, and I headed over to Franklin, New Jersey. Al developed a relationship with the organizers and came year after year to this small municipal fireworks celebration. Tagging along as a sort of interloper to observe this quaint event, I quickly realized my need to revert to a more practical skill set. Prices had changed a bit, and demographics had shifted along with people's tastes and expectations. As the sun began to set, money changed hands faster and faster. Customers wanted lights, and a line of kids formed at our tent. Teens were throwing snappers everywhere. The smell of funnel cake filled the air. The festival was alive, and then, the fireworks took to the sky. The momentum of commerce ground to a halt. Everyone craned their necks upward for a moment of stillness.

In that moment, I thought. I thought about how I was impressed with how adept of a saleswoman my teenage sister was and that my dad knew how to use digital payments. I thought about those long rides in the family van and those days when the sun felt unbearable as it bore down on us. I remembered in 2000 when my dad put on his own festival in Trenton. I remembered Grandma dancing with a hired clown. I remembered being proud even though it was a meager success at best. And I considered how the work we were doing didn't feel long for this world, a relic of an analog, non-search-optimized time, and I was glad I got to do it one more time with the people I loved.

THE NEW JERSEYEST SUMMER OF MY LIFE

By Mike Dawson

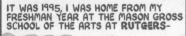

IT WAS 1995, I WAS HOME FROM MY FRESHMAN YEAR AT THE MASON GROSS SCHOOL OF THE ARTS AT RUTGERS—

I— WANT— YOU TO KNOW

THAT— I'M— HA-PPY FOR YOU...

AND I TOOK A NIGHT SHIFT AT THE DELI COUNTER IN THE RED BANK WAWA.

SOUPS   DRINKS

TUNA

CHIPS   SIDES

ITALIAN

MIKE

WHILE AT THE SAME TIME WORKING ALL DAY OPERATING THE "PARACHUTER'S PERCH" RIDE AT SIX-FLAGS GREAT ADVENTURE IN JACKSON.

WAWA WAS ALRIGHT, EXCEPT FOR HOW OFTEN FORMER NEMESES FROM HIGH SCHOOL WOULD STUMBLE IN DRUNK, MID LATE NIGHT BAR-CRAWL...

hurr hurr

LOOK, ITS DAWSON!

COFFEE

hurr hurr, MAKE ME A ROAST BEEF SUB, DAWSON

GREAT ADVENTURE WAS MONOTONOUS AND HOT, AND I WOULD BE TIRED FROM HAVING WORKED ALL NIGHT

DID I FORGET TO STRAP THOSE PEOPLE IN?*

WHEEEEEE!

* YES. A COUPLE TIMES. EVERYTHING WAS FINE THO

I COULDN'T KEEP UP THE PACE, AND QUIT BOTH JOBS AFTER A FEW WEEKS.

IS THIS SAFE?

MIKE

MY MOM HELPED ME GET A JOB AT A FARM PICKING JERSEY TOMATOES THROUGH ONE OF HER FRIENDS-

OH MY GOD...

THIS IS HARD!

IT WAS CASH UNDER THE TABLE, WHICH WAS GOOD, BUT I WAS FIRED AFTER A SHORT TIME FOR MOVING TOO SLOW.

BUT NOW I CAN'T HELP IT, WHENEVER I'M IN THE RED BANK WAWA OR GREAT ADVENTURE, I HAVE TO FIGHT THE URGE TO TELL WHOEVER'S WORKING THERE-

YOU KNOW, I USED TO WORK HERE TOO!

WARNING: SMOKING WILL KILL YOU

I'M SURE THEY FIND THAT FASCINATING!

41

The Golden Age of Bicycle Racing

MICHAEL C. GABRIELE

There was a strange occurrence in Orange, New Jersey, on Thursday, January 30, 1879. A man on a high-wheel bicycle rode along the chilly boulevards, waving to curious passersby. It was a sight few had ever seen, and according to a report in the town newspaper, it created "quite an excitement" on the usually quiet streets of this Essex County town.

"The main wheel, nearly five feet in diameter, upon which the rider's saddle rests, is composed of double spokes made from the finest steel," the *Orange Journal* reported on February 1, 1879. "The tire is soft rubber. There is a small balance wheel in the rear. The perfect ease with which this machine is propelled over our macadam roads indicates the useful purposes to which it may be applied. Our young friend, Llewellyn H. Johnson of West Orange, is the owner of the bicycle." Johnson became a sales agent for Columbia bicycles, a leader in Garden State cycling associations, as well an accomplished rider.

Four months later, on May 31 and again on July 12, 1879, the Short Hills Athletic Club of New Jersey hosted two-mile bicycle races. A network of bicycling enthusiasm had taken root throughout the Garden State. An article in the June 30, 1893, edition of the *New York Times*—with the headline "A Good State for Cyclists"—proclaimed that New Jersey "can justly boast of having the fastest bicycle rider in the world, Arthur A. Zimmerman, the best roads in the country and the prettiest bicycle clubhouses in the Union."

Top riders, superior infrastructure, and the grass-roots efforts of dedicated cycling clubs created the Garden State's legacy as the cradle of US cycling. Beginning as a national craze in the 1880s, cycling evolved as a major spectator sport and an international enterprise. World-class athletes from throughout North America, South America, Europe, New Zealand, and Australia all came to New Jersey. Sparked by the collective efforts of wheelmen clubs and sports entrepreneurs, the Garden State—Newark, in particular—was the hub for this burgeoning international sports circuit.

But for all the glory of New Jersey's golden age of cycling, it quietly faded from memory, and few remnants were left behind. It is a forgotten history.

New Jersey clubs promoted cycling as part of a healthy, family-friendly lifestyle and encouraged community engagement in the sport. Civic pride was on display in New York City on May 28, 1883, as cyclists from Orange, Newark, Hoboken, New Brunswick, Plainfield, and Smithville, bedecked in their colorful club uniforms, took part in a grand bicycle parade along

Racers at the Newark Velodrome, circa 1920. Courtesy of the Jeff Groman Collection.

Fifth Avenue. The procession stepped off at 3 p.m. with 750 cyclists riding in formation. Not to be outdone, Jersey City staged its own bicycle parade on August 29, 1896, a gathering of 1,500 riders that included 200 women cyclists.

Newark, Trenton, Vineland, Plainfield, Orange, and Asbury Park spawned bicycle clubs and sanctioned major races. Students at Princeton University formed a cycling club, as reported in the October 10, 1879,

Daily Princetonian. Rutgers College (now University) in New Brunswick also demonstrated its student cycling spirit. The February 29, 1884, edition of the *Rutgers Targum* reported that campus wheelmen had formed the Rutgers College Bicycle Club.

This groundswell of cycling popularity did not go unnoticed by New Jersey's business community. In the spring of 1897, a group of investors looking to seize upon the potential of cycling as a spectator sport, unveiled plans to create a wooden velodrome in Vailsburg (annexed by Newark on January 1, 1905). A corporation known as the New Jersey Bicycle Track Co. built the track. The Vailsburg board track, as it came to be known, was a quarter-mile oval, located on the south side of South Orange Avenue. It opened on May 31, 1897, with Arthur Augustus Zimmerman as the featured attraction. Born in Camden on June 11, 1869 (some sources say 1870), "Zimmy" was an established, international star who competed in cycling tours of Europe and Australia between 1892 to 1895. In August 1893, he took part in the World's Fair Cycling Tournament held in Chicago and became a world champion.

The buzz of the 1900 season at Vailsburg focused on a young rider from East Orange named Frank L. Kramer. Kramer, born in Evansville, Indiana, in 1880, made his professional debut at Vailsburg. He went on to become one of the greatest pro riders of the golden era. Kramer excelled at the Vailsburg oval and spent parts of the 1905 and 1906 seasons on tour in Europe, boosting his international reputation as an American star.

Two days after the close of Vailsburg's 1910 season, an article in the *Newark Evening News* marked the next chapter of New Jersey's golden era of cycling. The story announced plans for the construction of a new bike track, the Newark Velodrome, which would be built opposite the Vailsburg board track, on the north side of South Orange Avenue. It would become the crown jewel for the golden era of cycling, attracting the world's greatest racers. The Newark Velodrome—a one-sixth-of-a-mile oval track with a seating capacity of 12,500—opened on April 16, 1911. Frank Kramer dominated this venue, and his greatest victory in Newark came on September 2, 1912, when he won the pro world championship, defeating the top cyclists of Australia and Europe.

Alfred Timothy Goullet became another popular racer at Newark and competed often against Kramer. Born April 5, 1891, Goullet lived with his family in Emu, in the state of Victoria, Australia. In 1910, Goullet packed his bags and boarded a boat to the United States, wanting to race in Newark, which he called "the center of racing in America." By 1921, press reports in the *New York Times* frequently identified Goullet as "America's premier cyclist," "the all-around bicycle champion of America," and "the greatest all-around bicycle rider in the world." He retired in 1926 and continued to live in the Newark area, enjoying his status as an elder statesman of the bicycling game. He died in Toms River on March 11, 1995, just shy of his 104th birthday.

Pro cycling in New Jersey began to lose its luster in the late 1920s. Fans, riders, promoters, and journalists became painfully aware of the downward trend in attendance. Newark had lost its two star attractions, Frank Kramer and Alf Goullet, to retirement. After more than thirty years, the repetitive velodrome racing format had lost its appeal and no longer entertained crowds. Investment money ran dry to maintain the track and develop new riders. The public turned its attention to other sporting

Nutley Velodrome. From the collection of the Nutley Historical Society.

activities in the 1920s, such as car and motorcycle racing. Fledgling pro
football and basketball leagues were emerging, and Babe Ruth's exploits
for the New York Yankees reenergized major league baseball. Pro cycling
became "old news" on the sports pages. The October 30, 1929, edition of
the *Newark Evening News* reported that the 1928 and 1929 seasons were
"disastrous as far as business is concerned." The Newark Velodrome held
its final races on September 21, 1930.

In 1933, Joseph Miele, an East Orange entrepreneur and cycling
fan, stepped forward to fill the void left by the Newark Velodrome. He

announced plans to build a new velodrome in Nutley, confident that he could rejuvenate cycling. Miele signed the sport's top athletes from the United States and Europe to ensure that opening day would be a world-class celebration. The Nutley Velodrome opened on June 4, 1933, before a standing-room-only crowd of twelve thousand fans.

The famed American sprinter and Newark native Bill Honeman made his first appearance at the Nutley track on June 14, 1933, winning the one-mile pro race. Honeman landed in Nutley following a two-year stint of racing in Europe. He brought with him a stars-and-stripes silk jersey designed for him while he competed in France. The jersey became a national sensation and was adopted by the sport's governing bodies as the official racing jersey for US cyclists.

Nutley's operations were successful during the first two seasons, but attendance began to wither during the 1935 season. Financial and management problems soon followed. With bicycle races foundering, the December 17, 1937, edition of *Nutley Sun* carried a front-page story that said town commissioners had granted a license to run midget auto races at the wooden "saucer." The car races were popular during the 1938 season, but three fatal accidents at the track prompted Nutley to cancel midget car racing in 1939.

Nutley suffered the same decline in fans and ticket sales as did the Newark Velodrome ten years earlier, and Miele announced that he was prepared to shutter the venture. There was a final attempt to hold cycling at the Nutley track in the summer of 1940. Attendance dwindled to only a few steadfast fans, and the velodrome was in serious disrepair. The operations were no longer financially sustainable. The track closed its gates for the last time on September 15, 1940, and the golden era of US velodrome cycling had come to an end.

Frederick William (Pop) Kugler, a machinist, former bike rider, and cycling enthusiast, witnessed the demise of the velodrome era but envisioned new opportunities for the sport. In his younger days as an amateur cyclist, he competed in long-distance road races and became inspired by their potential as engaging athletic events. In addition, he took advantage of the freedom to experiment because cycling, as a national circuit, slipped into a lull. Velodromes were closed, and lionized pro riders had retired. Regional club teams kept cycling alive in New Jersey and elsewhere, but the ranks of top riders were slim.

Kugler used his many connections in the sport and lined up sponsors. He launched the first Tour of Somerville—a fifty-mile, closed-course, "criterium" race along the streets of Somerville—on May 30, 1940, attracting 137 riders. Furman Kugler, Pop's son, won the inaugural event. Later that summer, Pop Kugler packed up his car and drove his daughter, his son Furman, and young Harry Naismith to the US National Amateur Championship races, which were held August 30 to September 2, 1940, at Chandler Park, Detroit. Furman won the senior men's title, Mildred won the senior women's title, and Naismith garnered the men's junior title. Their victories received national press coverage and put Somerville on the map as a cycling center.

The second Tour of Somerville was held on May 30, 1941, and Furman again was the winner. Carl Anderson of Clifton won the tour's 1942 crown. The race was suspended from 1943 to 1946, due to World War II. Tragically, the two champions, Furman and Anderson, were killed during the war, and when the tour resumed in 1947, it was renamed the Kugler-Anderson Memorial Tour of Somerville.

Eventually, the Tour of Somerville became a festive Memorial Day weekend event and opened the competition to female cyclists. The Tour of Somerville remains the oldest race of its kind in the United States and serves as a link to the Garden State's enduring cycling legacy.

The golden age of New Jersey's velodromes ended eighty years ago, but bicycle racing evolved and is thriving as a global and Olympic sport. Rediscovering the Garden State's long-lost cycling heritage honors the heroes and pioneers of the past and provides a deeper appreciation for the sport's grand history for current fans and athletes. Today there are many club teams throughout the Garden State. Just as the *New York Times* observed nearly 130 years ago, New Jersey is "a great state for cyclists." It always will be at the heart of cycling's living history.

The Ultimate Bike Tour of Trenton

WILLS KINSLEY

If you had just one day to visit our fine capital city, this is the ride I would take you on. The route encompasses all wards and features some of my favorite stories from Trenton's deep history that I picked up from the over ten years I've been leading bike tours in town.

    This ride is roughly twelve miles and best completed on any bicycle with air in the tires and an adventurous and curious rider! It doesn't hurt to follow all traffic laws and give a ring of the bell and a wave to folks passing by either.

Turn by Turn direction key: \L\ = Left turn; /R/ = Right turn; |S| = Straight; |X| = Cross

    Start in Mill Hill Park. *{Head North on S. Broad St. then \L\ W. State St.}* Pass New Jersey's capitol building, the second-oldest State House still in use. The dome is covered with forty-eight thousand pieces of gold

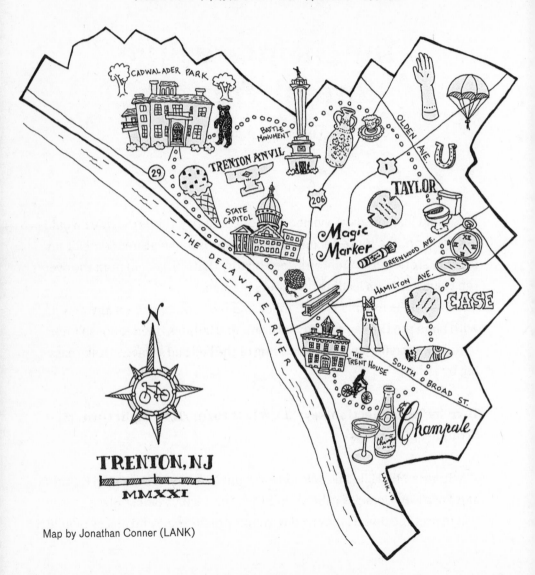

TRENTON MAKES ✶ THE WORLD TAKES

Map by Jonathan Conner (LANK)

leaf. Each piece of gold leaf cost one dollar and was paid for in 1999 with money raised by New Jersey school kids through the "Dimes for the Dome" program. *{/R/ Parkside Ave.}* Look up! You are passing underneath the Delaware & Raritan Canal State Park. Originally built for transport barges pulled by mules, its multiuse path can take you from here to New Brunswick or up to Frenchtown as it parallels the Delaware River. *{\L\ Cadwalader Park Entrance}* Take a loop in Trenton's "Central Park," designed by Frederick Law Olmstead. Stop into the Ellerslie Museum and keep an eye out for the gravestone of Briar Patch, once the oldest living black bear in captivity, who lived at the park alongside deer and monkeys. *{Exit the park |S| Bellevue Ave.}* The building at 20 Bellevue Avenue is the Higbee Street School (later known as the Nixon School), constructed in 1857. It was the first school specifically intended for Black children in Trenton. It is a great example of simple Greek Revival temple-form structure and is on the National Register of Historic Places. *{\L\ Calhoun St., then /R/ Pennington Ave.}* Up the road, you will see the Battle Monument, built on the location of George Washington's captured German cannons that fired downtown during the First Battle of Trenton; he now sits atop the 150-foot Roman Doric column. *{/R/ N. Warren St., then \L\ Perry St.}* You won't be able to miss the Trenton Fire Headquarters sign on your left. Stop into the Meredith Havens Fire Museum to see fascinating artifacts from one of the original firefighting forces in the US that began in 1747. *{\L\ N. Clinton Ave.}* On your right is the Taylor Ham Pork Roll factory, one of the two companies that produces New Jersey's favorite mystery meat (we'll see the other one soon). Many of Trenton's world-famous industrial potteries were located around this stretch of road. Ever use a urinal or toilet?

Yup, they were perfected right here, with many companies consolidating to become American Standard. *{/R/ N. Olden Ave.}* The Blacksmith of Trenton is on your left a bit down the road. It has been in operation since at least 1823. If the door is open, pop your head in! *{/R/ E. State St.}* Up the road to the left is the Switlick parachute factory. Thousands of lives have been saved by its parachutes, inflatable rafts, and life vests. *{\L\ Chambers St.}* Check out the new Trenton Central High, home of the Tornados, built in 2019. The original 1932 structure was one of the largest high schools in the US when it was completed. *{/R/ Morris Ave.}* Wetzel Field is to your left. Baseball great Babe Ruth hit a home run there that is still talked about to this day! *{\L\ Washington St.}* Keep an eye out for Case Pork Roll, family owned by the descendants of George Washington Case, the inventor of pork roll. Trenton has not one but two festivals where you can pig out on this homegrown delicacy. One egg, cheese, and hash brown for me, please. *{/R/ Liberty St., then /R/ Lalor St. |X| Rt. 29}* Riverview Cemetery is on your left just past Route 29. It is the final resting place of Trentonians from all walks of life, including Civil War veterans, former governors, and titans of industry the Roeblings, whose wire rope built the Brooklyn Bridge and the Golden Gate Bridge. *{/R/ Cass St.}* Waterfront Park is on your left; catching a game at Trenton's great minor league ballpark is always a great idea on a summer night. *{\L\ Centre St.}* Look out for a funky fence made completely of bicycles (built by yours truly) at the Boys and Girls Club Teaching Garden. *{\L\ Bridge St.}* The Trent House is on your left, home of Scottish businessman William Trent, who bought this land that would become his namesake town from the farmer Mahon Stacey. Trenton could have been Staceyville! *{/R/ Market St., then \L*

S. Warren St.} Soon you will cross the Assunpink Creek, which gets its name from the Lenni-Lenape language and means "stony water place." These original people were removed from their original Lenapehoking territory and forced west to what is now Oklahoma and Ontario, Canada. They were the first inhabitants who realized the beauty and potential of this land on "the falls" of the Delaware River. *{/R/ Lafayette St.}* You did it! This ride only scratches the surface of Trenton's rich history, so more adventures await . . .

Emily Thompson, *Tastee Sub Shop*, 8 × 8 inches, oil

On Immigration and Sandwiches

The Story of One Beloved Restaurant, One Central New Jersey Suburb, and One Child of Immigrants

POOJA MAKHIJANI

I

Tastee Sub Shop on Plainfield Avenue in Edison, New Jersey, is an unattractive Italian deli with blue clapboard siding, fluorescent lighting, and limited seating. Here, patrons order by number. The #7 is turkey breast, a choice of honey-roasted, oven-roasted, or smoked turkey. The #14 is all cheese (provolone, Swiss, and white American). The #5, the only sandwich that has a name (the "Super Sub"), combines pressed ham, boiled ham, capocollo, salami, prosciuttini, and a choice of provolone, Swiss, or white American cheese. The shop accepts credit cards, but diners receive 5 percent off their orders if they pay by cash. Tastee's unassuming appearance belies its iconic status in the region.

Tastee was founded in 1963 by George Thornton and Dave Caldwell and has changed hands only twice: in 1972, to David Thornton, George's son, and Carl Padovano and, in 2019, to Brian Thornton, David's son, and Steve Moraldi, who had worked in the shop since he was in high school. Although Tastee now has two other outlets in Central New Jersey, in Franklin Park and in Lawrenceville, the Edison location is the most well-known.

In July 2010, then-President Obama met with small-business owners, including David Thornton and Padovano, at Tastee's Edison shop and ordered a six-inch #5: "Super Sub with everything" (lettuce, tomatoes, onions, oil, vinegar, salt, and oregano) to go; at nearly forty-nine years old, Obama declared he could no longer eat the twelve-inch variety.

I had grown up in Edison and was visiting my parents that day. Our ranch house—which looked exactly like every other house on the street, down to the single tree in the same place in every yard—was my parents' first home in the United States. They had immigrated from India in the mid-1970s, lived in New York, and chose Edison to live their "American dream" because the township was affordable and offered easy access to New York City via New Jersey Transit.

Like many of our neighbors, my father and I walked to Tastee to catch a glimpse of President Obama. We saw road blockades, US Secret Service snipers, news vans, and both protesters—many waving the Gadsden flag, a favorite among Tea Party enthusiasts, an anti-Obama movement that gained prominence in government that November—and supporters, who were far more racially, culturally, and ethnically diverse by my observations. The president signed a paper bag upon his departure; the bag now sits under glass, in front of the shop's meat and cheese slicer.

II

The sub sandwich's origin story is murky and contested, but it's likely that what Americans know as "subs," or by any of their regional names, are a version of Italian sandwiches that came to New York through immigration at the turn of the twentieth century. Italian Americans have always been New Jersey's largest single ethnic group: upon their arrival in the late 1800s, they settled in urban centers like Jersey City and Newark and Paterson and Trenton and agricultural towns like Hammonton and Vineland.

Howard Robboy, professor emeritus at the College of New Jersey in Trenton, who wrote "The Socio-cultural Context of an Italian-American Dietary Item" as a sociology graduate student at Temple University, posits that southern Italian immigrants, nearly all of whom worked as laborers, from seamstresses to seasonal farm workers, folded Italian meats, cheeses, and seasonings into bread, creating a meal with familiar flavors that could be transported and eaten on the job. The sandwich grew in popularity with ethnic groups other than Italians, especially in the 1930s and '40s.

III

Outside New Jersey, Edison is best known for its most notable denizen—the scientist who invented the lightbulb here in 1876 in his Menlo Park lab—not for its sub shops. The township was, at that time, known as Raritan, but it eventually took the inventor's name. It was a quaint, rural town until the mid-twentieth century, when corporations such as Ford and Revlon, both within bike-riding distance of my childhood home, opened assembly plants. Workers flocked to jobs in Central New Jersey; they were mostly "ethnic" whites: Italians, Irish, Polish.

Edison's demographics dramatically changed from the 1970s to the 1990s. A wave of Asian immigrants arrived in New Jersey as a result of the Immigration and Nationality Act of 1965, which ended immigration-admissions policies based on race and ethnicity. Prior to this, restrictive immigration laws were designed to maintain a white majority in the United States and explicitly banned Asians. My father secured his visa to the United States after the passage of the 1965 law; my mother followed. A second surge followed after the passage of the Immigrant Control and Reform Act in 1986, which removed country quotas and educational and professional requirements for immigrants, allowing them to immigrate via lottery or family sponsorship. According to 2019 US Census Data, 48 percent of Edison's population is now Asian; only 36.8 percent is white.

IV

Some New Jerseyans consider I-195, which runs west to east from Trenton to Belmar, the unofficial dividing line between North and South Jersey. In North Jersey, an Italian sandwich is called a "sub" or "hero," if in closer proximity to New York City; in South Jersey, with its Philadelphian influence, the same torpedo-shaped sandwich is called a "hoagie." I've heard both "sub" and "hoagie" in Central Jersey, which, by my definition, lies on the I-95 corridor, bisecting the state northeast to southwest and connecting New York City and Philadelphia.

New Jerseyans quibble whether Central Jersey is a distinctive region of the state. In a December 2019 tweet, Governor Phil Murphy was compelled to write, "As Governor of the Great State of New Jersey, I hereby declare that CENTRAL JERSEY DOES EXIST," and he defined which counties constituted the region. Dan Nosowitz, in a widely shared essay in *Atlas Obscura*, declared, "In reality, there isn't anything especially different about Central Jersey," and disregarded its existence entirely. When a friend texted Nosowitz's piece to me, I shot back, "He's white. Otherwise, he'd know that Central Jersey is where people of color feel at home and in community." In 2015, NJ Advance Media mapped New Jersey's demographics using 2010 US Census data; what emerged was a pointillist painting of the state's diversity. The I-95 corridor shimmers orange, purple, and green, signifying "Black," "Hispanic or Latino," and "Asian," in stark contrast to the map's wide swaths of blue, marking "White," in the northwest and southeast. That white New Jerseyans don't, or can't, recognize Central Jersey's distinctive culture and that they continue to argue about it on talk radio and on internet forums is not surprising. Racism often makes the most obvious invisible.

V

As the only child of color in my classroom and communities through much of elementary school, I faced all sorts of racist microaggressions—mispronunciations of my name; assumptions about my parents' English-language abilities, despite the fact that they were college-educated in a country that was colonized by the English for two hundred years; teachers foisting Christmas celebrations on me. I desperately wanted to be white; then, it meant eating bologna on Wonder Bread or hosting birthday parties at the roller-skating rink. I lived a bifurcated life. At home, I spoke in my mother tongue, watched Bollywood movies, and found kinship with other South Asian American children from nearby towns, our chosen family. At school, I exaggerated my Jersey accent, learned cultural references that were, and still are, foreign to my family, and hid all traces of my cultural heritage.

The microaggressions never faded, but as the town became less white, the macroaggressions began. Businesses were egged, places of worship were spray-painted with swastikas and hate speech, and homes, including mine, were vandalized. Someone threw a jagged rock through our living-room window when the house was dark, sending shards of glass everywhere. That night, the police lieutenant said, "It was just some high school kids having fun."

I held these conflicting feelings—the desire to be white and a fear of whiteness—as many children of immigrants do: by ignoring them or holding them in, until they exploded, on the page for me, years later.

VI

Tastee became central to my aspirational whiteness but also to my family's eventual assimilation. The shop was open until 11 p.m. daily, and on many Sundays, my parents would pick up sandwiches for my brother and me to take to school the following morning, at my pleading. I think they saw it as convenience, nothing more, and they, too, were foodies—willing to try anything tasty. Subs were always ordered with oil and vinegar "on the side," to keep the crusty, soft bread from becoming soggy overnight, although the plastic containers of oil and vinegar often popped open in my backpack, leaving streaks of sweet-smelling condiments all over my textbooks.

The sandwiches were inextricably linked to one annual family tradition: a late summer day at the US Open tennis tournament in Flushing Meadows Park. Every year, for two decades of my childhood, to avoid the event's exorbitantly high food prices, we brought along our favorite Tastee subs accompanied by cans of Coca-Cola, stored in a cooler in the trunk of our car. At lunchtime, we would return to the car, parked in the shadow of the tracks of the 7 train; outside food wasn't allowed inside the venue. It was always Tastee subs we packed, never any other picnic foods. I always ate a #7: a honey-roasted turkey with everything and honey mustard, which was available on request.

VII

I left Edison in 1996. I moved to Baltimore, for college, then New York City, then Singapore, with my then-husband. Edison continued to change—and not.

Existing ethnic tensions played out in politics and civic life. In 2006, the town elected its first and only Asian American mayor, Jun Choi, the son of Korean immigrants who owned an Edison dry-cleaning business. During his campaign, the talk-radio host Craig Carton, who along with Ray Rossi were known as the "Jersey Guys," proclaimed that he did not "care if the Chinese population in Edison [had] quadrupled. . . . Chinese should never dictate the outcome of an election. Americans should." Also that year, Indian immigrants accused an Edison police officer of brutality during a Fourth of July incident. The officer was cleared, but the local Police Benevolent Association called for Choi's resignation. Ugly protests erupted. The *New York Times* referred to the furor as "not unfamiliar in towns with a fading industrial base and a disaffected, largely white, blue-collar population" and quoted Bill Stephens, a former councilman who ran against Mr. Choi in last year's mayoral race, who said that long-term white residents feared being forced from their own town: "I think there's a little thought of 'they're taking over and I'm being pushed out of my community.'"

The demographic changes continue. A Walmart superstore and an Amazon fulfillment center, now the town's largest employers, opened in 2008 and 2018 on Route 27, which bisects the township from north to south. The highway also serves as the route of the township's Lunar New Year parade. It's lined by Asian small businesses—restaurants, tax preparers, dentists—all with Mandarin or Gujarati or Vietnamese signage. The diner around the corner from my childhood home is now a hot pot restaurant, although its midcentury facade is still intact. An immigrant Uzbek family now lives in my childhood home.

My parents moved northwest, into bucolic Somerset County, in 2012. In 2016, after my decade-long marriage ended, my daughter and I chose to move in with my parents, as I leaned on them to help me raise her.

VIII

I still frequent Edison, although ironically, all these years later, I feel more at ease at Tastee and in Burger King, which is across Plainfield Avenue, or Sam Ash Music, across Route 27 and where I frequently bought music paraphernalia, than I do in Edison at large. At the sub shop, my New Jersey accent resurfaces when I order. It's at the wholesale Asian grocer in a former warehouse district where I feel out of place, even though the produce and spices on its shelves are intimately familiar to me. I'm thankful for the diversity. My elementary school has many children of color now, and I imagine a little Brown girl not feeling so isolated by her race and culture—but I also realize that I'm not wholly part of these immigrant spaces. I've assimilated too much, found myself too proximate to whiteness, if there is such a thing.

Recently, I picked up a six-inch #14 for my mother and a foot-long #9 (tuna salad) for my father and me. Even though I'm mostly vegetarian, I can't resist Tastee's tuna salad, made in-house every morning with only tuna fish and mayonnaise. All the restaurant's ingredients are sourced locally and delivered every day. High school students, mostly, prepare vats of lettuce, tomatoes, and onions daily, and meat and cheese is sliced to order. Tastee's menu hasn't changed in almost fifty years, although there are some off-menu items, such as a salad sub (no meat, no cheese), for those in the know.

IX

The United States is a suburban nation, with a majority of Americans living and working in this landscape. But the suburb is more than a physical location; it is also a social production: the suburbs have always been a site for the consolidation of white identity. They were designed to be all white *on purpose*.

The American suburb seems at a crossroads: across the country, 61 percent of immigrants now migrate to the suburbs, bypassing cities. More ethnic neighborhoods are now found in the suburbs than were inside city limits four decades ago. In Edison and elsewhere, the reshaping of the suburban landscape—often in very visible ways—has resulted in real struggles, which complicate questions of race, history, and identity.

It has been half a decade since I returned to Central New Jersey, and it's hard not to see the region as a microcosm for the rest of the nation. As of 2020, less than half of children in the US are white; by 2045, most people in the US will be nonwhite. Just like the suburb, the United States is also a site for the consolidation of white identity; it was designed to be white *on purpose*. This is the story of a beloved deli and a Central New Jersey town, but it's not a singular story.

KEANSBURG

by KAT SCHNEIDER

I GREW UP IN KEANSBURG.
BUT NOW THAT I THINK ABOUT IT, I DON'T KNOW IF "GREW UP" IS THE RIGHT PHRASE.
I LIVED THERE UNTIL I WAS ALMOST EIGHT.

KEANSBURG IS A SMALL, VERY BLUE-COLLAR SHORETOWN WITH ITS OWN BOARDWALK AMUSEMENT PARK
THAT I WAS NEVER ALLOWED TO GO TO...EVEN SO, I LOVED LIVING THERE.

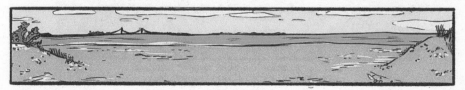

WE USED TO PICK THE HONEYSUCKLES OFF THE FENCE BETWEEN OUR CHURCH + THE NEIGHBOR'S YARD.

MY BROTHER + I WOULD RIDE OUR BIKES IN THE PARKING LOT BEHIND THE FIREHOUSE THAT WAS NEXT DOOR + PRETEND TO BE EMTs.

EMERGENCY MEDICAL!!

I GOT MY HEAD STUCK IN THAT PARKING LOT'S GATE ONCE...

(I DON'T REMEMBER HOW ...OR WHY.)

AS I GREW OLDER, I BEGAN TO REALIZE THE VARIOUS REASONS WHY MY FAMILY MOVED. I DIDN'T REALLY PROCESS THE WEIGHT OF THAT DECISION UNTIL YEARS LATER.

ONCE IN A WHILE I'LL DRIVE THROUGH THE TOWN, BUT THERE'S NOTHING LEFT FOR ME THERE.

NOW THAT I'M AN ADULT, IT'S FUNNY TO HEAR MY FIANCE'S FAMILY + FRIENDS FROM HOBOKEN TALK ABOUT HOW MUCH THEY USED TO LOVE VACATIONING IN KEANSBURG.

SOME OF THEM STILL GO EVERY SUMMER.

THE WAY THEY TALK ABOUT THEIR SUMMERS THERE FEELS THE SAME AS THE WAY I USED TO THINK ABOUT KEANSBURG WHEN I WAS A KID.

I'M ALWAYS HAPPY TO PRETEND FOR A LITTLE BIT.

Illustration by Joy Velasco

Why I Want My Son to Grow Up in Jersey

CHRIS GETHARD

Sometimes I wonder why it felt so important to me that I return to New Jersey to raise my son. There are the obvious answers: more space than you get in a city, closer to his cousins, great school systems. For as lovely as those things are, though, they don't quite quell the concerns that I carry with me as someone who grew up in the great Garden State during the '80s and '90s.

I love New Jersey. I love that I grew up here. But I think if you talk to almost anyone of my age group, we'd all agree that growing up here was, at times, quite scary.

From my hometown of West Orange, you could see the New York City skyline. That always seemed beautiful to me, until a teacher off-handedly said, to a classroom full of the final wave of Cold War kids, "You know, we're so close to New York City that if the Russians ever nuke it, we'd get at minimum third-degree burns in this town." (Don't even get me started on how my entire generation, Jersey or not, lived in constant fear that we were going to be abducted by Satanists in vans.)

In junior high, some kids from a neighboring town made a game of hanging out near our school after the final bell and jumping kids. They might take your Walkman or your pocket money or might just push you around for fun. Two friends of mine saw these kids across the street from school one day and went into the office to ask for help. They were told, "They're across the street. It's not on school grounds. There's nothing we can do." It was scary to realize that adults don't have your back.

The year before I entered high school, a kid hung himself. He would've been a sophomore. The school wouldn't let his family set up a scholarship in his honor. They wouldn't even let his picture go in the yearbook with his graduating class. It was scary to realize that the school's priority was to sweep something that awful under the rug instead of dealing with it or explaining it; instead of attempting to heal, they wanted to erase his memory from existence.

One night in college, I was at the Stone Pony, partying with a few friends. We'd booked a room at the Berkeley. This was before the pinball museum and the hip Korean tacos. This was when abandoned buildings stood half completed in the middle of streets. My friend Katie got too drunk, a college-kid mistake, and somehow it fell on me to carry her from the Pony to the hotel, right down the main drag. The younger set might be reading this thinking, "So what? Asbury Park's awesome." And it is. But anyone over the age of thirty remembers when you didn't want to spend too much time there at night, let alone while dragging a pixieish, blacked-out blond girl around. People shouted at me from under the board-walk. I really thought we were going to get killed.

It was scary the time I went to Paterson to pick up boxes from the warehouse of the company I worked for back then, and the skies opened up out of nowhere, filling Paterson with water like a bowl. I stood in a lot in an industrial part of town, surrounded by fencing and barbed wire, watching the water rise in front of me like a cartoon. I ran to my car, driving it into feet of water, wondering if the car would be disabled but not caring since I was keenly aware that a kid like me shouldn't spend a night on the streets of this area of Paterson.

It was scary to live here on 9/11 and the days after. Military jets flew over our homes, patrolling the skies. Much like the threat of third-degree burns that kept me up at night when I was a kid, there was that feeling that we were so close to someplace so big and that any time something went wrong, there we were right on the edge of that cliff.

It was scary to feel suicidal at a state university so massive that it was impossible for anyone with the ability to help to notice. (I pray that this has changed for Rutgers students who came after me.) It was scary to feel suicidal in a place that obsesses so much over toughness.

All these fears (and many others) mixed together and percolated and turned me into someone who, upon exiting childhood and entering adult-hood, could on my best days be considered "an anxiety-riddled mess who had his guard up at all times." It took me years to unwrap that.

I don't blame New Jersey for my problems. I have a messed-up head. I would have had problems if had I grown up anywhere. But do I think that this place, its culture, its location, its attitude, had elements that made my problems worse and not better? I absolutely do.

So if various experiences I had in the state scared me so bad, and if those fears added to my tenuous mental grasp so severely, why would I ever want to raise my kid here? Wouldn't the smart bet be to flee? Maybe to someplace that I have to assume is more peaceful, more calm, more *normal*, like I imagine—I don't know—Maryland or somewhere might be?

Well, here's the thing about growing up in New Jersey: for as scared as I was a lot of the time as a kid, I have spent very little time scared as an adult. Growing up in New Jersey, I think you get a lot of life lessons out of the way early on. (Most people would probably say "too early.")

When I first moved to New York City, I saw a lot of people who had also just arrived, from places like Michigan and North Carolina and Oregon. The sense I got was that they were being blindsided by the reality of real living in their midtwenties, while I stood there thinking, "They're reacting to things that I got used to by the time I was twelve." The idea that you have to work hard? I've known that forever. The idea that no one is going to look out for you if you don't know how to look out for yourself? Duh. New Jersey gave me a very good bullshit detector. I spotted hustles from farther away. I knew how to swat away the entreaties of people testing what they could get out of me, from grifters on the street and in professional situations as well. The smoke-blowing, promise-making weasels that look to attach themselves to you? More often than not, I've seen them for what they are pretty early in the process.

I was once walking home from the subway and got a call: a very famous comedian had booked a show at the Forest Hills tennis stadium, and he forgot to book an opening act. The person on the phone had heard I lived in Queens and was wondering if I could get there within half an hour. Twenty-five minutes later, I was onstage by myself under a spotlight performing in front of over twelve thousand people. I don't think I'd have had the confidence to walk onto that stage if I wasn't from New Jersey.

I've hosted shows on live television. I've traveled all over the world staging shows for audiences full of strangers. I've revealed things about my past and my personal life on public record that most people would say you should keep behind closed doors.

Being an entertainer isn't a hard job; it's cushy. I'm not claiming to be a coal miner or anything. But you do wind up in over your head a lot, facing down weasels often, put in situations where a lot of people are spending tons of money and need things to move fast. There's pressure and judgment from all sides. As a long-recognized anxiety-riddled mess, I've certainly felt those pressures and judgments, but I've never let them mess with my head in the same way I often see among my peers. And I really think I owe that to New Jersey.

Because New Jersey can be scary. It can be harsh. It makes you grow up way too fast. It can fill your young head with information you probably shouldn't know. But it also teaches you a simple fact that we know better than people from most places: life's a game, and you're allowed to play it.

I want my son to know that, in his bones. The idea that we might as well get in the ring and see what happens because we've already seen some shit in this world? I think that's a fire all Jersey natives have in their guts when they are young and are only able to verbalize when they're a bit older.

And like all games, we know life is there for the taking. If you're smart and thick-skinned, you might even manage to win. And even if you don't, losing's not as scary as the things you learned when you were a confused kid and teachers told you the world might melt at any moment. Life is hard, confusing, and unpredictable, but to Jersey people, it's not all that alarming.

I mean, it's certainly not as scary as Route 22 at rush hour, but that's a whole different matter.

Garden State Breakfast Pie

STACEY MEI YAN FONG

This Taylor Ham / Pork Roll egg and cheese pie is made with a poppy-seed crust and topped with salt, pepper, and ketchup. The crust is divided down the middle, so you can pay homage to the iconic Jersey breakfast debate— use Taylor Ham on one side and Case's Pork Roll on the other.

Ingredients

Crust

1¼ cups unbleached all-purpose flour

½ teaspoon kosher salt

1½ teaspoons granulated sugar

1 tablespoon poppy seeds

¼ pound (1 stick) cold unsalted butter, cut into ½-inch pieces

½ cup cold water

2 tablespoons cider vinegar

½ cup ice

Illustration by Kasey Bohnert

Filling

4 slices of Taylor Ham Pork Roll (sliced to ⅛-inch thick or your desired thickness)

4 slices Case Pork Roll (sliced to ⅛-inch thick or your desired thickness)

8 slices of American cheese

6 eggs

salt

pepper

ketchup

Equipment

10-inch pie plate

Aluminum foil

Ceramic/metal pie weights—an alternative is using dried beans, rice, or sugar

Pastry brush

Directions

Crust

1. Stir the flour, salt, sugar, and poppy seeds together in a large bowl. Add the butter pieces on top of the dry ingredients.
2. Use a pastry blender to cut or rub the butter into the ingredients until it is in pieces a bit larger than peas (a few larger pieces are okay; be careful not to overblend).
3. Combine the water, cider vinegar, and ice in a large measuring cup or small bowl.

4. Sprinkle 2 tablespoons of the ice-water mixture over the flour mixture. Using your hands or a spatula, lightly toss the mixture until the water is incorporated. Continue to add the ice-water mixture, 1 to 2 tablespoons at a time. Carefully mix until the dough comes together in a ball, with some dry bits remaining.

5. Turn the dough out onto a lightly floured surface. Knead dough together till it comes into one mass. Be careful not to overknead. Shape the dough into a flat disk, wrap in plastic, and refrigerate for at least 1 hour or preferably overnight.

6. Place your pie pan in the freezer for 10 minutes. After 10 minutes, grease your pie pan with butter. Then using foil, build a divider in the center so that you can make two crust compartments when blind baking.

7. Take your dough out of the fridge. Lightly dust a work surface with flour, and lightly dust a rolling pin. Roll out the dough to about ¼-inch thick, rotating it as you work to help prevent it from sticking. To transfer the dough to the pan, gently roll it up, wrapping it around the pin, then unfurl it into the pie plate. Make sure to get your pie dough lying flat into the pie plate and into the two compartments you have made. You can do this by lifting the excess dough around the edges, giving the dough some slack, and using your fingers to push the dough down into the pie pan.

8. Next you are going to crimp the edges of the pie dough. Start by using scissors to trim away the excess dough, leaving about ½-inch excess all the way around the outside edge of the pie plate. Tuck this excess dough under, pressing gently to make it flush with the edge of the pie plate. Crimp the edges of the pie dough into your desired shape.

9. Once you have crimped the edges, use a fork to prick all over the bottom and sides of each compartment. This step is called "docking." Docking helps eliminate the air bubbles that can form when the dough is exposed to heat and also prevents the crust from shrinking. Place the crust in the freezer for 15 minutes.

10. While the crust is in the freezer, position the oven racks in the bottom and center positions, place a rimmed baking sheet on the lowest rack, and preheat the oven to 425°F. Make your egg-white glaze by mixing 1 egg white with 1 teaspoon of water. This glaze acts to moisture-proof the crust that will be exposed to the filling. It's not totally necessary but does make for a better final product.

11. When the crust is frozen solid (about 15 minutes), line it tightly with a piece or two of aluminum foil. Make sure the crimped edges are completely covered and there are no gaps between the foil and the crust.

12. Pour pie weights or whatever alternative you are using into each compartment in the crust concentrating around the edges of the compartments. Place the pan on the preheated baking sheet and bake for 20 minutes, until the crimped edges are set but not browned.

13. Remove the pan and the baking sheet from the oven, lift out the foil and pie weights, and let the crust cool for a minute. Use a pastry brush to coat the entire crust with a thin layer of the egg-white glaze (1 egg white whisked with 1 teaspoon of water) to moisture-proof the crust. Return the pan, on the baking sheet, to the oven's middle rack and continue baking for 3–5 more minutes. Remove and cool completely before filling.

Filling and Baking

1. Preheat the oven to 400°F
2. Make four small cuts around the slices to prevent them from curling. Fry the slices of Case Pork Roll and Taylor Ham until crispy and warmed through.
3. Make sure your blind baked crust is baked and cooled. On one side, layer Taylor Ham with the American cheese, till that section is full. Do the same on the other side with Case Pork Roll and American cheese.
4. Bake in the oven till the cheese melts, about 10–12 minutes.
5. While the cheese melts between the ham in the oven, hard fry the eggs.
6. Once the cheese is melted, take the pie out the oven and top with eggs, salt, pepper, and ketchup
7. Serve and enjoy!

Interview with Stacey Mei Yan Fong

What is 50 Pies, 50 States?

The project is an ode to the country I have chosen to call home. I have decided to bake fifty pies, each one representing each state and its culinary trends or history. I started the project when I was in the process of applying for my green card / permanent residency in the US. I wanted to learn more about my new country. The United States is huge! And the way people talk, the landscape, the climate, and the cuisine vary so much across the whole country. It's really incredible and super fascinating. I had been to a lot of places but still had a lot more to visit. I feel one of the fastest and easiest ways to experience a new place is through food.

Why pie?

I can't think of anything more American than pie. It is the ultimate dessert comfort food in my mind. This quote from the TV show *Pushing Daisies*, "Candy might be sweet, but it's a traveling carnival blowing through town. Pie is home. People always come home," really resonated with me. It is also one of the few desserts that translates well as a savory dish, so the possibilities with pie were endless!

How do you approach your research?

I start each state by determining if I know someone from there. Conversation is often great way to get the ball rolling. Then I scour the internet and find out if the state has particular state vegetables/fruits or a local delicacy that is really only eaten there. I look at the big picture and think about how I can adapt a state's foods into a pie, whether savory or sweet. When I got to New Jersey, I thought immediately of two things: Taylor Ham and fat sandwiches.

Had you been to New Jersey at that point?

Yes, many times, to visit friends that live near Lake Hopatcong, and I had been to Jersey City and Montclair. I went through Newark Airport in college on my way from Savannah to Hong Kong.

Do you think you had any expectations of what New Jersey should be like before you went?

Growing up, I listened to Bruce Springsteen a bunch, so in my mind, Jersey was just Asbury Park and the shore. At that time, I hadn't watched *The*

Sopranos yet, so I didn't know anything about North Jersey. I feel that New Jersey has so much wilderness and beautiful lakes that people don't talk about much. I did a small portion of the Appalachian Trail that goes through New Jersey for roughly thirty miles, and it was gorgeous. I saw my first black bear cub in Jersey. Sometimes it's nice to go in with kind of an idea of what you think a place is and then have your expectations exceeded.

How did you decide what to bake for your New Jersey pie?
The state fruit is northern highbush blueberry, so at first I was like, maybe I'll do a blueberry pie. Then I remembered college friends from Jersey who would always tell me about fat sandwiches, and I considered that. But my most vivid memory was waking up at the aforementioned house in Lake Hopatcong, and my friend's brother made everyone Taylor Ham egg and cheese sandwiches on an everything bagel, and it hit me: I have to make a pie like that! I remember he explained to me how to cut the slashes in the ham so it doesn't curl when you fry it, and I obsessed over the packaging: I thought it was so retro and beautiful. As I talked to more people from the state, I found out about the Taylor Ham versus Pork Roll debate, which is why the pie ended up spilt into two compartments. I wanted to make a divide down the middle and play up how people in the same state call it different things.

Did you have to drive to New Jersey to get the meat, or do they sell it in NYC?
I couldn't find it in New York! My coworker Amy, who lives near the shore, brought me some Taylor Ham, and my friend Liz, whose family lives in

Ewing, brought me a huge roll of Case's Pork Roll. It took a whole state coming together for me to assemble my ingredients.

What was the reaction when you served the pie to your New Jersey friends?

It was pretty much completely demolished in like fifteen minutes. People got a kick out of me dividing up the crust. It was really nice to get the approval from people that are from the state. Sometimes it feels like a shot in the dark, trying to honor a state's culture as someone on the outside.

Photo by John Vigg

The Only Bar That Matters

An Oral History of the Original Asbury Lanes

KAMELIA ANI

Asbury Lanes was a bowling alley opened by Ed and Kay Ayles in 1985. In the 1990s, it was put into eminent domain by the city of Asbury Park and then purchased by a big development company. In 2003, a band of creatives and general misfits got together and had this crazy idea of turning this mostly abandoned mom-and-pop bowling alley into a punk-rock music venue. Kay Ayles and her son Ralph turned over management to them. Asbury Lanes was born out of both boredom and a growing need for a place the weirdos of Asbury Park could call home. It was a bar, bowling alley, and music venue that hosted punk shows, art markets, sex-toy bingo, burlesque shows, country music, and more. It almost didn't make sense that this place could be so many things, but for some reason, it worked.

When I first walked into Asbury Lanes, it was to collaborate on a documentary about the Lanes with a photographer I met while working on my own photography project, "Humans of Asbury Park," where I set out to photograph and interview residents and visitors to the town. He was shocked that I had never been to the Lanes before. While I had made many acquaintances in town, I was still a twenty-seven-year-old Orthodox Jewish mom struggling with my own identity and place in life. I had my feet in two different worlds and didn't quite fit in anywhere. I thought I would be so entirely out of place at a punk-rock show in a bowling alley. But as I walked into the Lanes in my skirt and wig, camera in hand, I immediately felt a sense of acceptance in this strange world I had entered. What came after that first night can only be described as a transformative love affair between this place and me. Every person I have ever met who stepped foot into the Lanes has a similar story to tell. The Lanes became known fondly as "The Only Bar That Matters," and I came to know this to be true.

Jenn Hampton, manager of Asbury Lanes (2003–15): I was thirty and living on Long Beach Island at the time and was asked by some friends to come help with this project they had just undertaken. When I first drove into Asbury Park, I thought, "What the heck is this place?" Everything was boarded up. There were lots of shady people hanging out on the streets. Nothing was really open, just one or two bars, a couple of stores and art galleries. It was pretty desolate. The first time I walked into the Lanes, I didn't quite get the vision. It was so run-down and so unloved, like a reflection of the town. But the idea was to have this sort of bowling alley that was magically locked up and reopened as if nobody had touched it for forty years. My friends who roped me into the project wanted it to be styled after the Googie architecture of the 1960s, and we worked hard to make everything in the bowling alley look older than it actually was to match that theme. There was an overall circus theme as well. You could see it in the color choices of teal-blue tiles and orange furniture. At first, I had thought I was just working on a renovation project; but the universe had other plans, and eventually I moved here to do Asbury Lanes full-time.

Pete Steinkopf, guitarist for The Bouncing Souls: At the time that the Lanes started doing stuff, Asbury was pretty dead. It gave people a place to come and share their ideas with each other, a local creative community. And that's what Jenn was all about, and the Lanes was an extension of her. It just kind of exuded into the world through her.

Angie Sugrim, lead singer of The Obvious: Asbury Lanes was like a suburban arts and culture place, but our weird version of it. When it opened, the town was a lot less populated. You could kind of do whatever you wanted within reason, and no one would stop you.

Mike McLaughlin, house photographer of Asbury Lanes (2004–15): I guess I was thirty-six. I was a contract photographer, and I got an assignment from the *Ledger* telling me there's this place in Asbury Park, and they're doing this oldies car show thing, and they've got music. So I went down to Asbury Lanes at like three in the afternoon, and I met a bunch of the people and talked to them outside because I was taking pictures of the cars. And then I went inside, and I met Jenn and Sasquatch, and the Sickibiliies were playing. I literally just walked around meeting the people.

Photo courtesy of Blur Revision Media Design

I swear to God, there was just something . . . At that point in my life and my career, I had been in a million bars, a million music venues. I had been to numerous bowling alleys. And I swear to God, when I walked in there, something in my head was like, "You're home. This is home."

Zach Moyle, lead singer of Lost In Society: I was like fifteen or sixteen years old the first time we heard about Asbury Lanes. We thought, "We gotta check this out." We went to go see either The Ergs or The Loved Ones. At that point, I was still pretty new to going to shows. And we walked into a bowling alley, so I had no idea what to expect. We walked into a time capsule from the '60s. Nothing was changed, except it was punked up.

Shannon Brown, Lanes regular: One of the first shows I remember going to at Asbury Lanes was The Bouncing Souls in 2007 or so. I had just broken my hand, and a friend offered me an extra ticket. I had never heard of the Lanes before, but when I walked in, I thought, "All right, I know most of the people here, so this is probably going to be a cool place." It was comfortable. It felt like I'd been there a million times before. I ended up sitting on the stage. I was hooked.

Mike: Everyone called it a punk club, and they had tons of punk bands there. But they also had a ton of marching bands there! So you could call it a marching band club. They had tons of rock, tons of rockabilly. . . . You always had a different audience, mixed with the regulars there. The music, the people were odd and different and open, and that was the thing: it was always the Island of Misfit Toys.

Angie: My record release for my band The Obvious was on my actual thirtieth birthday. I got my friends' bands to play, and it was like I got the biggest birthday party ever. And my band got to play too. We had just done a record with Pete from The Bouncing Souls, so that was super exciting. When I say it back, it almost doesn't sound real how cool it was. Another of my favorite nights there was when The Germs played there, and Pat Smear, who was in Nirvana for a minute, was there. And that was the cool thing about the Lanes: there'd be people like him, like the dude from The Clash and Kathleen Hannah, in this setting that was like someone's house almost. That's how intimate it felt.

Pete: Our old drummer had left, and we didn't tell anybody we'd been working on getting a new drummer. So the day before, we dropped the surprise and advertised that we'd be playing at the Lanes. We had no idea how many people would show up, and when we got there, there was a line around the corner. It ended up being a crazy wild show, and it was one of the most memorable nights there.

Shannon: You could walk in crying, and someone was bound to come over and say, "Okay, something happened. Here's a beer. Here's some tater tots. Here ya go. When was the last time you ate?"

Zach: The Lanes wasn't cool because it was an old bowling alley. It was cool because the people working there knew what to *do* with an old bowling alley. I mean, going on tour and playing hundreds of shows at smaller

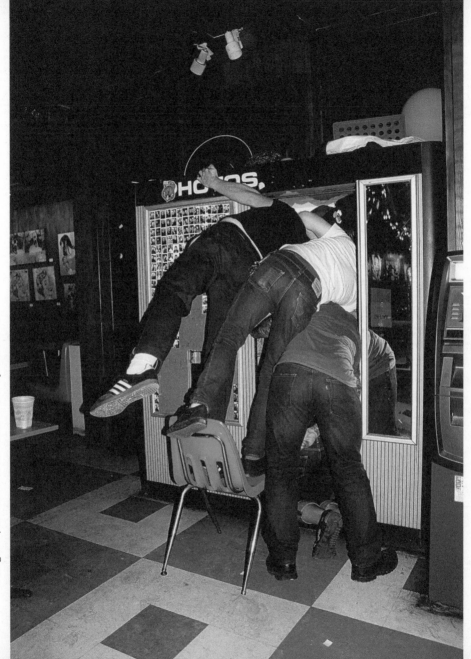

Piling into photobooth at the Lanes. Photo by Kamelia Ani.

venues like the Lanes, there were only a few that can even compare. And it's not because of the space or the sound; it's because of the people.

Angie: You know when you're in school and you're riding bikes around the neighborhood and you end up at somebody's house? It felt like that.

Jenn: For a long time, because the building was put into eminent domain, there was this romantic notion that it wouldn't always be there. It was special because at some point we quit believing it would end. The magic was the collective sheer will of people to make it happen. Any time you have people that love something beyond a paycheck, you're always going to get that kind of synergy. There's always this element of, "We did it because we wanted to, not because we had to." The Lanes was special because there wasn't a boss or anyone to say, "No" or "This is bad."

Mike: Even when the heat would be broken, the lights would be terrible, the sound would be shit, and you'd still go and have the time of your fucking life.

JB, doorman and bartender (2011–15): It was pretty grimy. It had character you can't replicate.

Shannon: Years ago, I was sitting on the steps of the Lanes, talking to Joey Cape from the band Lagwagon, and he said that everybody who walked into those doors left a piece of themselves inside. And because of that, it had its own life force. We were talking about the Lanes closing at that point, and he said it would be nothing short of murder. He was right.

Angie: Those nights were the best, where you said, "Okay, I'll just go out and have two drinks." And then you met some band from South Carolina who ended up crashing at your friend's house, and you stayed up all night to show them sunrise at the beach. And then there were nights when people fell asleep in the parking lot, like, on the ground . . . but everybody lived to tell the tale.

JB: Even at towards the end, Asbury was changing a lot, but the Lanes was kind of the last stronghold of weirdos.

Mike: In 2003, when the Lanes opened, there wasn't a lot going on. It brought a lot of people in, and it created a whole community. And a lot of those people either moved to Asbury because of it or opened up businesses in town. People came to the Lanes and felt that sense of community and they wanted to make it their home. That played a huge part in the resurgence [of Asbury Park]. The shame of it is that any time you have any kind of resurgence or gentrification, people want to come to a place because of the cool kitschy kind of vibe or whatever and love it for its edginess, and then they move here and fuck it all up.

Jenn: I hear so many stories like, "If the Lanes never existed, I wouldn't have met x, y, and z, and I wouldn't have this business, or I wouldn't have this husband, or this wife or this job." . . . Apparently, everybody can get a

Photobooth strip from the Lanes. Courtesy of Rachel Casey, Allyson Dwyer, and John Teehan.

job based on their connection to the Lanes except me [*laughs*]. I really do think, though, that that's the biggest devastation: that I realized in the moment that these things happened and people had these experiences and took them outside these walls, and it triggered something. And that's creation. And somehow this place hosted it. So what does that mean? It's emotional to think that's how synergy works. It worked great when everyone there had the same intentions. It only got fucked up when you had people coming in who didn't want to do what everyone else was doing. And that's what iStar did.

[*In 2015, the development company iStar took over Asbury Lanes. It reopened in 2017, keeping the name and nothing else.*]

Pete: I always walk by there to get to the beach, and I always have these déjà vu moments, or like I can almost see us all hanging out the back door smoking and talking and hanging. There were hundreds of nights like that for six or seven years.

Zach: I know it's selfish, but I miss playing there. I miss that being our home base. Any time we had a record release or a hometown show, it was without a doubt going to be at the Lanes.

Mike: I haven't found a venue I like shooting at since the Lanes closed. Obviously, there was a lot of sadness and all, but it was like lightning in a bottle. And something like that can only exist for a small amount of time.

Jenn: I don't want the Lanes to be the greatest thing I've done in my life, but it's hard to top all the things I got from that experience. I don't know how to transition out of that.

Mike: Before the new Lanes opened, everyone was reaching out asking if I was going to go, and I said, "If they bring Jimmy Hendrix and Joe Strummer back from the dead for a duet, I'd consider it. And not even a definite for that." I won't go there because it would be disrespectful to my memories. The fact that they kept the name and they try to pretend that it's still Asbury Lanes, when they have nothing to do with Asbury Lanes and kept nothing from it, it's disrespectful. When I was interviewed for a documentary we were working on, they asked me what I'd like to see happen to the Lanes when it closed. And I said, "I'd like to see it blown to fucking pieces in a giant fiery ball because that's the only thing that would do justice to its legacy."

Zach: I'm passing judgment because it was my favorite place in the world, and now it's some corporate shell. It's like an airplane hangar. There's no life behind it. The thing about the old Lanes was the people. I have life-long friends from that place. I don't think you can copy that or force that kind of camaraderie. The new place opening was like reopening a wound. They asked us to play before they officially first opened the new Lanes.

Photo by Kamelia Ani

They wanted us to headline one of the first Saturdays there and offered us a pretty good amount of money, but we said no. It was like, "Fuck you guys. You put our friends out of work. You took this place from us."

Pete: It's none of the same people, not the ones who work there or the ones who go to see shows there. Asbury Lanes was *the* neighborhood bar. And this is not that.

Angie: I don't think the Lanes as it is today is meant to fill the void left by the old one. Asbury's on the map now. That energy you have right before something gets really big, that moment has passed. The old Asbury Lanes was the center of that build or crescendo. The Lanes that exists now wants to be a destination for people, but it's not a two-way street anymore. They're a venue, and you can go there and buy what they're selling. But the old Lanes, you could go there and say, "I think I have something to contribute." You could participate. It was a collaborative. You can't get that from this place, and this place isn't here to give you that.

Jenn: It would be like going to a funeral and seeing a loved one's corpse over and over again. It's a weird way of describing it. I've gone through a lot of mental anguish over losing the Lanes. I went to a woman who is a spiritual therapist of some kind, and she said, "You have to go back into the Lanes. Even if it's in your brain. Because you gave so much of your heart there that there's a piece of it stuck in there, and you're never going to get over it. You've given so much to this place, and you're going to be stagnant if you can't get that piece of your heart back."

Shannon: I can't make myself do it. I've walked past it. I have considered going to shows, but I can't tarnish that memory. The last night I walked out of the Lanes was the last night that they were really open. And I walked out and watched them shut the lights, and it was the closure I needed. I can't walk through those doors again.

Why Did the Salamander Cross the Road?

KATE MORGAN

By the time the answer occurred to him, Dave Moskowitz was already standing in the mayor's office, waving a dead salamander around. Moskowitz, an entomologist and chair of the East Brunswick Environmental Commission, was on an early-spring walk in 2003 when he "came across a slaughter of spotted salamanders on Beekman Road." A quick investigation revealed vernal pools—shallow, seasonal ponds—in the woods just off the road.

To Moskowitz, it was clear what had happened: on the first warm, wet nights of spring, the salamanders tried to cross the busy road to reach their spawning ground. Based on the number of dead, it seemed like only a handful made it to safety. "I grabbed a road-killed spotted salamander and a live one, and I went over to the mayor's office to show him and say, 'We have to fix this.'"

When the mayor agreed and asked for solutions, Moskowitz could only think of one: "We'll have to close the road."

Illustration by Julie Benbassat

Every year since, on mild, moist nights in late February and early March, a roughly mile-long stretch of Beekman Road closes to traffic, yielding to chubby, six-inch-long amphibians. The creatures are a type of mole salamander, black with bright yellow spots, and can live for thirty years or more.

They lay their eggs in the pools each spring. "Then the adults leave the pond and mosey into the upland habitat, where they spend the rest of their life cycle. Year after year, they come back to breed," Moskowitz says.

Bathtubs of Biodiversity

Spotted salamanders aren't the only creatures reliant on vernal pools. In fact, the pools, which range in size from "a bathtub to a half acre," says

Moskowitz, are a microcosm of New Jersey's intense biodiversity. "In our pools alone, we have the spotted salamanders, wood frogs, spring peepers and chorus frogs, eastern newts, and gray tree frogs. We've seen snapping turtles and box turtles, and that doesn't even get into the vast number of aquatic insect species."

Vernal pools—so named because they appear in the spring, filling with rainwater and melting snow—provide safe habitat for species to reproduce. Because the pools dry up as temperatures climb in the late spring and early summer and are inhospitable to fish, there's very little predation of eggs and breeding or juvenile animals.

There are seventy-eight reptile and amphibian species that call New Jersey home, says Brian Zarate, senior zoologist with the state's Division of Fish and Wildlife. What happens at the vernal pools, he adds, "is an amazing story because you have this group of amphibians that, over the course of their evolution, have figured out that because vernal pools dry up for some portion of the hydrologic cycle, they're devoid of some of the predators you find in other water bodies."

It's a niche environment, Zarate says, "where mole salamanders and a couple frog species figured out that if they lay eggs at the right time, they can develop before it dries out and have fewer worries about predators eating the eggs and babies. The animals don't know this, but their genetics do."

It's part of what makes vernal pools such vital habitat to maintaining the state's native and naturalized species; in fact, there's more biodiversity in New Jersey's vernal pools than in most any other ecosystem in the region. But wildlife aren't the only ones who benefit from preserving the pools and the area around them.

"People should care about vernal pools for their own sake, too," Zarate says. "They collect snow runoff and spring water. When big development projects go in, like they constantly are in New Jersey, engineers have to find places for water to go so it doesn't end up sitting in people's basements and yards. Well, vernal pools naturally function that way. They're the original retention basin."

It's a fact that's long been recognized by conservationists and land planners in New Jersey, Zarate adds. "We were one of the first states to have protection for vernal pools, going back close to twenty years ago. It's still rare to have those protections at all."

A Species Superhighway

Despite being the fifth-smallest US state in land area and the most densely populated, New Jersey boasts a diversity of ecosystems, ranging from the rocky bluffs of the Delaware Water Gap to the pine barrens, the meadowlands, and the marshes, bays, tide pools, and estuaries along nearly eighteen hundred miles of shoreline. It's this diversity of habitat that makes the state so hospitable to so many animals: more species can be found in New Jersey than in Yellowstone National Park.

There are part-time residents, too. In the spring and fall, New Jersey is a rest stop on the species superhighway. In a massive migratory path that spans from the Arctic to South America, the state is a perfect layover point.

Around October, birds of prey including hawks, kestrels, ospreys, eagles, and owls fly over in the thousands, bound for winter hunting grounds as far south as Brazil. Other migratory birds of varying shapes, sizes, and species make the same trek. Cape May County, where the migrating masses like to stop and rest before crossing the Delaware Bay, is known as some of the best bird-watching territory in the country.

Just offshore, seals, whales, and fish like striped bass and tuna swim south in the fall, then pass by again, headed the other way, in the spring. One of the most impressive annual migrations is the march of the monarchs; the butterflies descend on New Jersey every year, en route to overwinter in Mexico.

Creatures that fly and swim don't encounter too many obstacles on their migratory routes. That's not the case for animals moving along and, in the case of the salamander, across roads and through developed areas. "The fragmentation of our landscape through development and our dense road network has limited their ability to move to new places," says Zarate. Development tends to displace animals, but it's not always as simple as relocating. "When they're confronted with the turnpike or Route 78, for instance, it really limits the ability to move in response to the loss of these critical habitats."

Crossing Guards for Critters

Beekman Road runs past small neighborhoods, with dark, wooded stretches in between. "A road with forested habitat on both sides will have salamanders in conflict with cars," Moskowitz says. "When a car and a salamander interact, the salamander loses."

It's not that drivers are unsympathetic; the salamanders are almost entirely black, and they stay still until after dark. They typically migrate to the vernal pools over the course of two or three rainy nights, "moving in a mass," says Moskowitz. "They're hard to see. But each female can be headed to the pool with one hundred eggs, so each one that's hit is a major blow to the population."

To predict the nights when road closures will be necessary, Moskowitz says he and his colleagues on the environmental commission have to think like salamanders. "When they'll move is related to soil temperature, the previous seventy-two-hour period's ambient temperatures, humidity, and rainfall. Early spring, warmish rains and high humidity are a trigger."

Though Beekman Road is relatively well traveled, Moskowitz says, "there's never been a single bit of pushback on closing the road to save the salamanders. It's become part of the fabric of our community." For the families of East Brunswick, it's become a highly anticipated annual event. "We don't just close the road," Moskowitz says. "We close the road and invite the entire community to come out." Spectators are invited to bring flashlights and walk—carefully—along the road and the edges of the vernal pools, spotting salamanders.

"To me, the greatest value is that we've got these families and kids having this wonderful nature experience I don't think they could get anywhere else, out on a road on a rainy night witnessing something that's happened for millennia," Moskowitz says. "I don't know how you measure the value of what a family takes away from it, but I've always felt like it must stick with them. We get so many people we've had to have the police direct traffic. Families with flashlights and umbrellas and rain boots are out walking along, bending down like they're picking up shells on the beach."

Moskowitz hopes this "social nature event" will continue to foster camaraderie between the residents of East Brunswick and their amphibian neighbors. Affection, after all, breeds protection. "We're supposed to be stewards of our backyards," he says, "of our town, of the nature around us."

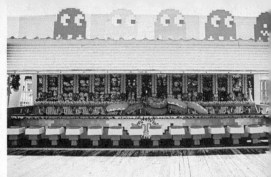

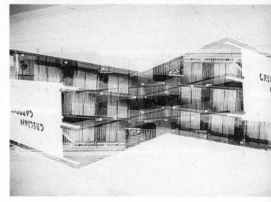

Photos by Katie Reynolds

Exit 0

BRITTANY COPPLA

Many people believe the Jersey Shore is a chalked-off patch of beach that has "Welcome To" and "Safe Travels" signs at its entrance and exit. The true Jersey Shore, though, is a chained colony of beach towns that knot like seaweed around your ankles, spanning along 140 miles of the state's coastline. Regardless of where you go—Asbury Park, Point Pleasant, Ocean City, Atlantic City, Cape May—the exit to your destination will rib off the Garden State Parkway, which braces the state like a spine.

In August 2009, my parents closed on a home in Wildwood, New Jersey. I was thirteen years old and spent much of that summer learning how to conceal a tampon string within my bikini bottoms while, an hour and a half away, an agita of Italian American twenty-somethings drank, self-tanned, and smushed their way through Seaside Heights. It was the last summer when the name Snooki might have been confused for the name of a candy bar.

Getting to Wildwood simply required following the parkway so far down until the highway itself becomes the exit, funneling from four lanes to three to two, before landing at the stoplight that marks the arrival of exit 0. I've never not known exit 0 as a legitimate, desirable destination, but I imagine an outsider who has been provided these directions and their likeliness to question, "Where will I arrive when there is nowhere left to go?"

In 2009, eight strangers took exit 82 off the Garden State Parkway to Seaside Heights. The only personalities who were actually from New Jersey were Sammi Sweetheart and Deena, a season 3 addition. The rest were primarily from New York, with the exception of the Rhode Island native DJ Pauly D.

Jersey Shore's primary plot documented the blotted reality of these vacationers living in a world unbound from time, sobriety, responsibility, self-respect, and abstinence. The episodes captured an endless loop of gym montages, swampy dance floors, bar fights, breakups, and black-and-white gyrating bed comforters filmed by remote-controlled cameras. Within the first four episodes, JWoww cheats on her boyfriend with Pauly D; a love triangle erupts between Sammi Sweetheart, Ron, and The Situation; Angelina voluntarily leaves the show after she abandons her shift at the Shore Store T-shirt shop; and Snooki is socked in the face by a man at the bar.

I was in seventh grade when *Jersey Shore* premiered. I didn't necessarily watch it religiously as it aired but made a point to be up-to-date. The series premiered in December 2009, the same month I got my first period in algebra class. Season 2 kicked off a month after I had my first kiss in an empty movie theater during a date I was driven to by my mom. In season 3, while Ron was hauling Sammi's bedframe to the porch and defacing her belongings during yet another breakup, I had my heart broken by a boy I thought I loved who, I realized many years after the show's filming, was both physically and emotionally abusive to me. It's a tragic cliché that I lost my virginity the summer after the series finale but the truth nonetheless.

In August 2015, I moved to North Carolina for college. I was eighteen years old, and *Jersey Shore*'s series finale had aired nearly two years earlier. Many people I met in North Carolina told me they knew I was from New Jersey the moment they met me. The unkind ones proclaimed it within minutes of our introduction, laughing at their detection of my home as if it were a punch line to a joke I didn't know I made. The more sensitive ones, though, would qualify their assumption, "but it's not because you're anything like the people from the show." This happened with people who had never visited New Jersey or even the US, when I lived in England for a semester, and it happens now that I live in the Midwest.

Every time, my reflex is to defend myself, to distance myself as much as possible from JWoww, Sammi, Deena, and Snooki. These women, and the many unnamed women who passed through the show's subplots, collectively formed an amalgamation of what it means to be a Jersey girl. To all the people I met in North Carolina and England and am meeting now in Chicago, I am a woman who will always exist in relation to these ballooned, dimensionless characters: ones who woke up each morning with stale breath and missing underwear, who dated and dated and dated horrible men, who were steadfast sites of violence and stupidity. But as much as *Jersey Shore* shaped the country's—the world's—perception of stereotypical women from New Jersey, it also shaped a world that expects this kind of woman of me.

I watch *Jersey Shore* every time I leave home again. I watched it in college with my best friend, one whose contact in my phone today is still "Meatball," the nickname Snooki and Deena coined for each other in season 3. I watched it when I studied abroad in Bath, then watched *Geordie Shore*, the infinitely more disorienting British remake of the original. I watched it the summer I exchanged New Jersey for Chicago.

Each time I restart the show, I think, "This will be the time I finally hate it." Because I want to. I want nothing more than to hate a show about a version of New Jersey that doesn't exist and faux natives who relapse into my home state every time summer returns. But the more capable I am of recognizing how predisposed the show's characters were, specifically the women, to violence, abuse, reduction, and artificiality, the more assured I am that I will return to it again.

One of the cultural contributions that *Jersey Shore* is undercredited for is its vernacular. Of all the jargon—"grenade," "cabs are heeeyah!," "smush," "T-shirt time"—the most notable linguistic consequence of the show is its invention of "DTF," or "down to fuck." I can only think of one boy who honestly asked me if I was DTF. It happened on a rooftop around 2 a.m., and we were close enough to the boardwalk to see the Ferris wheel's iridescence coat the lip of the sky. I said no, even though there was a full moon, which made me wish I were.

The acronym DTF is a condensed version of an already-lazy saying. The phrase can be shaped into both a question and an answer depending on the inflection. The acronym is unflinching in establishing what, exactly, a woman's role is. There was only one means of assessing how valuable any woman was to Mike, Vinny, Pauly, and, on occasion, Ron: her willing-ness to have sex.

The women of *Jersey Shore* established an equally colorful set of idioms throughout the seasons. The opening credits play candid sound bites of the cast while LMFAO's "Get Crazy" unspools in the background. JWoww's "After I have sex with a guy, I will rip their head off" and Sammi's "I'm the sweetest bitch you'll ever meet" are the two most artificial mot-tos, never actually shown in context on the greater show. Each time the show begins, Snooki cranks her neck backward on the "bitch" of her decla-ration, "I'm going to the Jersey Shore, bitch!" Deena triangulates her hands below her breasts and heaves them up as she asks, "You like the boobs?" Even in these isolated bites of the women's dialogue, there is no context that can make their characters anyone other than women who have sex and are, otherwise, bad. At the start of every show, the girls confirm what is about to happen; whatever profanities are preparing to ransack their bodies, this is what they asked for.

The memory I give myself the least permission to remember happened in Wildwood. I was seventeen years old, and my parents let me bring my boy-friend down the shore for a long weekend. He was the first boy I had sex with and the first one who told me he loved me in person instead of by text message. I remember how excited I was for the pictures, employing my younger sister to take endless photos of us on the beach, at the boardwalk, before dinner. I couldn't wait to have those photos to look at once the trip was over. I was excited to archive the person I wanted to see myself as: a high school girl in her favorite place with the first boy she loved.

One afternoon, my mom took my younger siblings to the water park, leaving the house unchaperoned for the day. As she buckled my brother and sister into the car, my boyfriend and I glacially applied sunscreen and packed a beach cooler, bottle by sweating bottle, waiting for their departure. As soon as the car pulled out of the driveway, we went up to my bedroom and took off the few clothes we were already wearing.

I was belly up when he took out his phone. He was still in his boxers, standing between my feet with his knees pressed into the bottom edge of my mattress. His thumb hovered over the camera icon and landed on it without consequence. He leaned his elbows onto the bed, steadying the phone so it rested on the mattress between my knees. The angle captured parts of my body from vantage points I had never considered. I had never wondered how I would look from between my legs. I never considered how, from that view, I had a body that was capable of appearing torn, halved by a neat slice that runs from my front to my back, separating my left leg from my right without a clear point of reunion. I never considered what I looked like from the ground. I shifted in uneasy but barely perceptible ways, hooking my toes inward and squeezing my thumbs between my fists.

I didn't protest that I hadn't consented to this, that I had never sent a nude and did not trust where those photographs could find themselves. I couldn't understand why he would want such unflattering photos of me when my tangible body was available to him whenever he asked, but I didn't try to source his justification. This wasn't the first time he had me pinned beneath the eye of his camera; it had happened before in his bedroom, in my basement, once in the woods, several times in the back of a car. But when I remember now that this was a thing that happened to me, I am always brought back to its instance in Wildwood.

I don't remember exactly what I said while he captured these photos of me, coiling into myself as soft and sure as a salted slug, but I know the preservation of my face seemed, at the time, like the biggest sacrifice. The way he captured me made it feel as though this were something I was expected to want.

The *Jersey Shore* house was laced with thirty-five remote-controlled cameras that did not shut off once throughout the course of filming. In the middle of the night, the cast members could hear the whirring of the gears as the cameras pivoted, manipulated by a crew wired in a few blocks away and archiving every moment of their lives throughout the two months it took to film a season.

I imagine how it felt for the girls to broadcast their bodies for over three years. I wonder how the cameras made themselves known in small but haunting ways to the women. I imagine Jenni on the night when she returned from her home in New York after breaking up with her boyfriend. Hours earlier, she was reclaiming her dogs—whom the boyfriend left alone to die—and tallying the items her ex brought with him when he abandoned their home. Now, she lies in bed, and a cry is curdling in the base of her throat, pickling her nose and eyes while she stifles it. She knows that lifting her hands to wipe away tears will only draw the cameras' attention.

I imagine Sammi in one of the many instances after Ron has flung her belongings on the patio outside their room. She bends down to recover a skirt, a tank top, an untied bikini bottom, a broken comb. She kneels and holds onto her laundry like a prayer. It is a relief for her, I imagine, to step outside in those hunched moments, when the stationed cameras cannot witness her pain.

The cast rarely acknowledges the cameras. There are few shots throughout the series when, amid the lawlessness, a member of the entourage breaks the fourth wall and confirms that if we, the viewers, are going to be instigators of this wreckage, we might as well witness it. But there is a moment in the final season when JWoww breaks the contract between herself and the conventions of reality TV. She is on the phone with Roger, her boyfriend, whom she has not spoken to in four days after he flung her by the neck at the club. When he did it, he cupped his hand below her jaw line, lifting her like the boardwalk claw machines as they claim the necks of the stuffed animals below. Jenni sits on the lumpy, red beanbag chair, and her legs are bent like a spider's. She grips the phone with such desperation that it distracts from the fact that the receiver is shaped like a wooden mallard duck, and then she asks Roger if he is leaving her. In the interlude between her question and his verdict, she looks toward the camera. In these seconds of her, I am reminded of faces I have been confronted by from across crowded rooms, looking toward a doorway set just behind me, pining for the arrival of a person they painstakingly need. Each time I watch this scene, I am surprised by my realization that she is locking eyes with the person holding the camera.

When my high school boyfriend took his phone out, I didn't consider the women from the show and the brutalities they accommodated. I don't think he considered his invasion of my body as anything other than an extension of what I already had coming. Belly up under that sunlight, I was just another Jersey girl, proven by a camera.

Signs I've Been Meaning to Read

SEAN RYNKEWICZ

Nearly every town in New Jersey has a historical marker or commemorative plaque designating something interesting that once happened there. Next time you pass by one, instead of thinking, "I've been meaning to read that," this is your sign to actually stop. Here are a few from around the state to get you started.

THE PLENGE
ARCHAEOLOGICAL SITE

•••

Nearly 13,000 years ago, groups of hunter-gatherers entered the Musconetcong Valley. Near this location is one of the most intensively revisited encampments of these early Native Americans or Paleoindians, ever documented in New Jersey. Thousands of stone tools recovered from investigations at Plenge provide a unique record of human lifeways at the end of the last Ice Age and reveal how Native Americans adapted to a changing world.

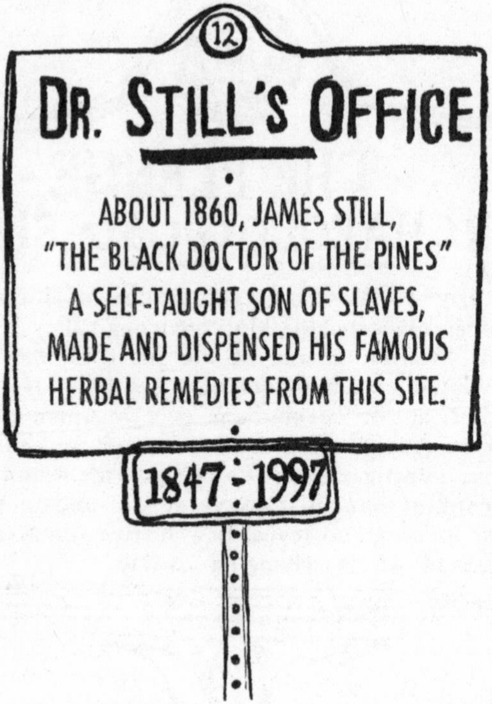

12

DR. STILL'S OFFICE

·

ABOUT 1860, JAMES STILL,
"THE BLACK DOCTOR OF THE PINES"
A SELF-TAUGHT SON OF SLAVES,
MADE AND DISPENSED HIS FAMOUS
HERBAL REMEDIES FROM THIS SITE.

·

1847 ÷ 1997

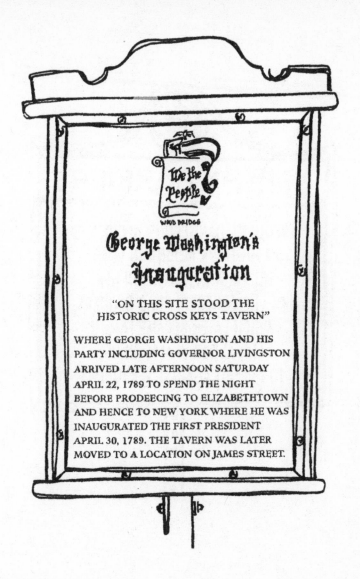

We the People

WOOD BRIDGE

George Washington's
Inauguration

"ON THIS SITE STOOD THE
HISTORIC CROSS KEYS TAVERN"

WHERE GEORGE WASHINGTON AND HIS
PARTY INCLUDING GOVERNOR LIVINGSTON
ARRIVED LATE AFTERNOON SATURDAY
APRIL 22, 1789 TO SPEND THE NIGHT
BEFORE PRODEECING TO ELIZABETHTOWN
AND HENCE TO NEW YORK WHERE HE WAS
INAUGURATED THE FIRST PRESIDENT
APRIL 30, 1789. THE TAVERN WAS LATER
MOVED TO A LOCATION ON JAMES STREET.

JERSEY BARRIERS

FREQUENT DANGEROUS ACCIDENTS
ON JUGTOWN MOUNTAIN LED TO
THE FIRST INSTALLATION HERE
OF THE CONCRETE ROAD DIVIDERS,
WHICH LATER BECAME FAMOUS
AND ARE NOW ALSO IN USE
TO DEFEND AGAINST TERRORISTS.

RINGLING MANOR - 1916

PRE-REVOLUTIONARY PETERSBURG
FORGE, LATER THE SITE OF
ALFRED T. RINGLING ESTATE.
CIRCUS ACTS AUDITIONED IN
MANSION. ANIMALS AND CIRCUS
EQUIPMENT OFTEN HOUSED IN
OUTBUILDINGS.

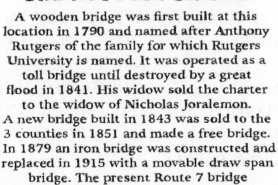

THE RUTGERS BRIDGE

A wooden bridge was first built at this
location in 1790 and named after Anthony
Rutgers of the family for which Rutgers
University is named. It was operated as a
toll bridge until destroyed by a great
flood in 1841. His widow sold the charter
to the widow of Nicholas Joralemon.
A new bridge built in 1843 was sold to the
3 counties in 1851 and made a free bridge.
In 1879 an iron bridge was constructed and
replaced in 1915 with a movable draw span
bridge. The present Route 7 bridge
was built in 2003 by the New Jersey
Department of Transportation.

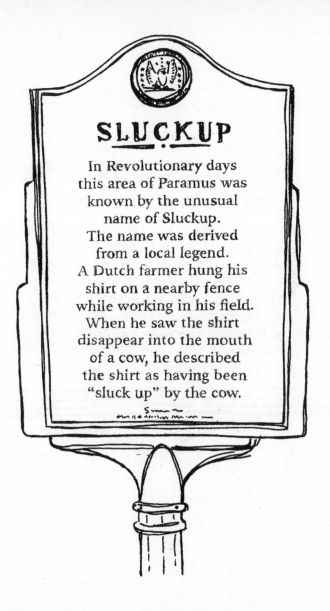

SLUCKUP

In Revolutionary days
this area of Paramus was
known by the unusual
name of Sluckup.
The name was derived
from a local legend.
A Dutch farmer hung his
shirt on a nearby fence
while working in his field.
When he saw the shirt
disappear into the mouth
of a cow, he described
the shirt as having been
"sluck up" by the cow.

VAN WICKLE
POTTERY c. 1828-1850

In 1824, Nicholas Van Wickle purchased
400 acres at Turtle Gut on the south
side of the old Manasquan River Bridge.
He established his pottery at this site.
Plain grey stoneware decorated with
blue hoops and simple brushed designs
of flowers and leaves was made here.
This stoneware was characteristic of Central
Jersey pottery produced during this era.

Me and *Mary Murray*

SCOTT NEUMYER

It's the spring of 2000, and *Mary Murray* has been rusting away in former merchant mariner George Searle's shipyard for the past twenty-four years. The once mighty and beloved ferry boat has become a wreck of her former self, a ghost with peeled paint and rusty holes in her hull. Time has had its way with her and she's fading away in a muddy swamp beside the New Jersey Turnpike.

It's the spring of 2000, and we've made it through the Y2K scare without seeing our bank accounts suddenly drop to zero or needing to sustain ourselves with endless supplies of canned beans and tuna fish from our underground bunkers. Summer is almost here, and it feels like we could be anything. Bruce Springsteen hasn't released a new album in five years, but his music still flows through the veins of Jersey folk like fresh, cold beer.

It's the spring of 2000, and teenagers are getting ready to spend their days laid out in the heat, soaking up the sun at the Jersey Shore. I'm not, though. I'm home from college, sitting in my childhood bedroom with the phone at my ear and tears streaming down my face. I am broken. Once useful and strong and attractive, I am a ghost. If I were made of metal

The *Mary Murray*. Photo by Peter Barlow, AIA.

rather than squishy human guts, I'd be rusting too. I'd be wasting away in my room while *Mary Murray* dies a slow death in the murky waters of the Raritan River.

It's the spring of 2000, and I will spend the bulk of my sophomore summer collapsing into a shell of my former self in ways I never thought possible. I will spend countless hours sobbing in the driver's seat of my Honda Accord while listening to Jersey bands like Senses Fail, Saves the Day, Midtown, and Catch-22 to try to save my sanity, while I hope time will rewind so I can take my now-ex girlfriend to that formal, so I can stay in Scranton, so I can keep my eyes focused where they should have been all along, so I can show her the respect she deserved and remind her of the past four years. I will lose more weight than I've ever lost in my entire life until I am gaunt and lighter than I was in high school. I will run until my lungs burn, Chris Conley's lyrics tearing my insides apart as I gasp for every breath. I will put hundreds of miles on that Accord making multiple trips back to Pennsylvania to prove I have changed. I will search high and low for secondhand cleats to send her. I will take her to see New Found Glory, leave the mosh pit nearly concussed, and end up waiting for her after the show in a ripped tank top, outside of Tink's, for nearly an hour, freezing in the cold Scranton night air, wondering what she's still doing inside. I will call her daily, even when I have no idea someone else is there by her side, and then, even when I do. I will play tennis and eat healthy and buy more concert tickets and arrange my own birthday trip to the city with her. I will spend my twenty-first birthday drinking too much, stumbling through crowds while crossing Fifth Avenue, and helping her pick out underwear that she will wear for him. I will drive in circles around the block until I know she's home to drop off home-made cassette tapes I had promised to drop off. I will convince myself that this is all okay because we are still best friends. I will cry until my eyes are dry, completely tapped out, while wondering why this is all not enough. All this while *Mary Murray* waits in vain for George Searle, who purchased her at auction in 1976 for $25,000 and towed her from Staten Island to his property in East Brunswick, to give her the makeover he's long promised.

It's the spring of 2000, and the only thing that snaps me out of my abysmal state is a visit from my friend Peter. He barrels through my bedroom door, refuses to listen to my protestations, and tosses me in the passenger seat of his 1984 Isuzu Trooper, where I will become a staple fixture for the next two months. We peel out of my parents' gravel driveway and into the sweaty darkness of a New Jersey summer filled with anxiety about the state I'm in and what we're about to do to fix it. We spend the days and nights speeding up and down Route 18, Route 130, Route 35, Route 9, the Garden State Parkway, the New Jersey Turnpike, and hundreds of local roads. We are armed with only our cameras, handed down from our fathers, loaded with rolls of expired black-and-white film that we will eventually develop ourselves. Our pockets are empty, save for a few bucks for gas or chai tea at Cafe 52. This is exactly what I need.

It's the summer of 2000, and Peter and I have pointed our cameras at waterfalls and animals and rusty bicycles left behind in the woods of Central New Jersey. We have trudged up sandy hills and down mucky banks and into the thick brush alongside Dunhams Corner Road, where an abandoned house once stood before it was erased in the name of a Community

Arts Center. We have balanced on fallen logs and scooted across creeks to find the remnants of the long-abandoned Turnpike houses near Middlesex County College. Peter has become the rudder steering me out of the darkest place I've ever been in. Like George Searle, he has rescued me from being dismantled. He has moored me in a new reality.

It's the summer of 2000, and Peter suggests we go on one last adventure. He tells me that we're not going far but that I should pack my camera, wear long pants and a dark shirt. He tells me that we probably shouldn't be doing this, that we don't want to get caught, and that we'll have to traverse through some thorny brush. He tells me, however, that it will all be worth it.

It's the summer of 2000, and we are plucking thorns out of our pants and looking around to see if anyone has spotted us. They haven't, so we loosen up, pull out our cameras, and make our way across George Searle's massive yard. We see *Mary Murray* in the distance, floating silently in the Raritan. She is just as beautiful and broken as we had imagined. We pass an old Texaco rig and plod carefully onto the small barge where she's moored. I tell Peter this was the best idea he's ever had, even though my heart won't stop racing. I'm terrified that we'll be caught, but it doesn't stop me from checking my aperture, twisting my manual lens to focus, and clicking the shutter over and over again. We are careful—*Mary Murray*'s body is worse for the wear and doesn't seem capable of holding our weight—but we take turns photographing each other and the ferry. We change rolls of film and keep going until we've had our fill, the memories of this mystical New Jersey mainstay forever burned into our minds and the emulsion on our film.

It's the summer of 2000, and there is no hope for the once-majestic *Mary Murray*. She will never be what George Searle hoped she would become—a floating restaurant (like one of her sister ships, *Miss New York*), a museum, an artificial reef. In eight years, he will tell the *Star Ledger* reporter Patti Lapone, "I was going to put a restaurant on the Hudson River. I was young and dumb at the time." I know the feeling, George.

It's the summer of 2000, and in nineteen years, *Mary Murray* will be dismantled piece by piece and sold for scrap, her leftover detritus floating wistfully to the bottom of the Raritan. George Searle will pass away shortly after at the age of eighty-one, a merchant mariner, honorary doctor, and decorated Korean War veteran, with only a few pieces of *Mary Murray* still resting on his East Brunswick property but the hopes and dreams of what she could have been in his heart and mind. I think this is for the better.

It's the summer of 2000, and just like in every good Springsteen song, there *is* still hope for me. It's right around the corner, mere months from materializing in front of my eyes at a late-night party in a friend's backyard. There is hope on the horizon. As long as I wipe away the tears and open my eyes for long enough to see it.

New Jersey Black History Sites

JACQUINN SINCLAIR

New Jersey might be best known for its beautiful shoreline towns and copious diners, but it has plenty more to offer, particularly in relation to history. There's the African American Heritage Museum of Southern New Jersey, which houses a collection of photographic portraits of wealthy Black families from the Victorian era. There are Black cemeteries where war heroes rest. Underground Railroad stops are up for exploration, and there are stately houses and social clubs where prominent African Americans once lived, celebrated, and worked. Here's a small sample.

Harriet Tubman Museum, Cape May

Illustration by Mikhaila Leid

In the early 1850s, the fearless slave liberator Harriet Tubman (born Araminta Ross) resided in Cape May, where she worked in the hospitality industry and for local families to save money for her rescue missions. With its proud promenade and beckoning beach, the quaint town was abuzz with abolitionist activity at the time and played a significant role in the fight for freedom. Located inside the Howell House, the Harriet Tubman Museum pays homage to its namesake and nods to the unfolding historical events of the time that took place in the vicinity of the building.

The T. Thomas Fortune Cultural Center, Red Bank

Freed by the Emancipation Proclamation of 1863, T. Thomas Fortune was a gifted writer and civil rights leader who rose to prominence as the editor and owner of a Black newspaper that underwent several name changes before finally settling on the *New York Age*. Fortune remained at the paper's helm for two decades and continued to print content that pushed back against the heinous treatment of Black people. Fortune's staff included such notable writers as Victoria Earle Matthews and the famous Ida B. Wells. Fortune went on to author a book, found the Afro-American Press Association among other organizations, and pen speeches for his good friend Booker T. Washington. Fortune moved to Red Bank in 1901 and bought a house that he called Maple Hall. The large home where the Fortunes entertained Black socialites of the early 1900s now is a cultural center that features Fortune's writings, hosts events that highlight the contributions of key African Americans, and offers tours. The home was placed on the National Register of Historic Places and named a National Historic Landmark in 1976. In 1979, the house was listed on the New Jersey Register of Historic Places.

Afro-American Historical Society Museum, Jersey City

On the second floor of the Greenville branch of the Jersey City Free Public Library, Afro-American Historical Society Museum visitors can view various periodicals, books, and other African American memorabilia. There's a replica of a 1930s kitchen, plus information about the Underground Railroad, historic Black churches, the civil rights movement, the Pullman porters, and more.

Illustration by Mikhaila Leid

Hinchliffe Stadium, Paterson

In the 1930s, Black sports fans crowded the ten-thousand-seat Hinchliffe Stadium to watch Negro League Baseball teams try their hand at victory. The art-deco-style stadium, one of few left from the era, has been owned by the Paterson Public School system since 1963. In its prime, Hinchliffe was the home stadium of the New York Black Yankees and the New York Cubans. The Black baseball stars Monte Irvin, Josh Gibson, and Satchel Paige all played on the field.

The African American Heritage Museum of Southern New Jersey, Atlantic City and Newtonville

Portraiture, furniture, materials showcasing Black stereotypes like "Little Black Sambo," and memorabilia from the Atlantic City boardwalk of a bygone era are just some of the exhibits in this museum's permanent collection. There are changing exhibits, too, at the African American Heritage Museum's two locations. The museum's nine-thousand-piece collection was born out of founder Ralph E. Hunter Sr.'s love of compiling historical objects, artifacts, and art.

Peter Mott House Museum, Lawnside

Lawnside was the first independent self-governing African American community north of the Mason-Dixon Line, according to the borough's website. Lawnside was formed after two settlements, Snow Hill and Fair Haven, merged.

Born in Delaware, Peter Mott was a husband, preacher, and local leader who bought a parcel of land in Lawnside and constructed his two-story house around 1840. Later, leading up to the Civil War, Mott worked to free slaves as a conductor on the Underground Railroad. The Lawnside Historical Society fought to preserve, acquire, and maintain the Peter Mott

House. The organization received the deed of the property in 1992. By 2001, the Peter Mott House was open to the public.

Mt. Peace Cemetery, Lawnside

More than seventy African American Civil War soldiers are buried at the Mt. Peace Cemetery. One soldier, John Henry Lawson, received the Congressional Medal of Honor for his bravery on board the USS *Hartford* during successful attacks against Fort Morgan on August 5, 1864. Mt. Peace is reportedly home to an additional three thousand people, including former slaves and others who could not be laid to rest at all-white cemeteries. The burial ground spanning eleven acres was organized in 1890 and is considered one of the state's largest Black cemeteries.

Krueger-Scott Mansion, Newark

The successful southern entrepreneur Louise Scott was the last owner of this looming Victorian-era house built in the late 1800s. Scott was a domestic worker who later started a chain of successful beauty salons in the city and ran her cosmetology school, the Scott College of Beauty Culture, from her mansion. Scott is believed to be one of the city's first Black millionaires. According to the Preservation New Jersey website, the home, formerly owned by the rich German beer maker Gottfried Krueger,

Illustration by Mikhaila Leid

later became the Scott Cultural and Civic Center. There are plans to re-develop the Krueger-Scott mansion into a mixed-use development with housing, commercial, and retail space.

Scotch Hills Country Club, Scotch Plains

For more than forty years, the Scotch Hills Country Club was known as Shady Rest Golf and Country Club. It was purchased in 1921 by a group of Black investors who organized Shady Rest, the first Black owned and operated golf and country club in the country. The popular club featured a nine-hole course, horseback riding, and a shooting range. Shady Rest was a gathering place for the Black elite and hosted famous musicians including Count Basie, Billie Holiday, and Duke Ellington.

In 1931, Shady Rest became the home of the professional Black golfer John Matthew Shippen Jr., who worked as the groundskeeper. Shippen competed in several US golf championship tournaments and worked at golf clubs up and down the coast. Shippen taught rich white club members such as the steel magnate Henry C. Frick and the former New Jersey governor J. S. Freylinghuysen and was also part owner of a now-defunct course he designed in Maryland. Shippen lived in a farmhouse on the property, which was built in the 1700s. The farmhouse is open to the public and features relics from Shady Rest's past.

Cemeteries

African American cemeteries, many of which have Revolutionary and Civil War soldiers resting there, can be found throughout New Jersey. Some are well preserved and marked, while others suffer from disrepair and lack signage. Here are a few to consider:

- Pennington African Cemetery, Pennington
- Stoutsburg Cemetery, Hopewell
- Butler Cemetery, Camden
- Mount Pisgah African Methodist Episcopal Church and Memorial Hill, Lawnside
- Midway Green Cemetery, Aberdeen

State Prerogatives

CARLOS DENGLER

My brother and I used to chuckle at an old New Jersey tourism commercial whenever it came on the television. Even back in the '80s, it seemed quaint to us Queens boys watching from Elmhurst, New York. Presented by New Jersey's then-governor, Thomas Kean, the commercial had an air of make-believe around it, full of crashing waves and rolling hills and a lilting piano underscore, as the governor—sporting khakis and an ivory cable-knit V-neck and dropping his *r*'s like some castaway from the JFK era—frolicked along pristine shoals, looked into the camera, and, with sincerity, spoke about his state's varied landscape ("A vacation in America, the Beautiful, . . . only smawlluh"). At the time, my brother and I were ensconced in an outer-borough version of New York City's infamous urban decay. TV and radio, however, made ignorance of the greater tri-state region impossible. Although we believed the commercial (we knew full well that New Jersey was one long expanse of sand, trees, and lawns), it nonetheless played against our ingrained skepticism, steeped as it was in grit and asphalt, about pride in anything but this survival contest here in New York, with the inevitable conclusion that all of those crashing waves, just a short drive away, might as well have come from Narnia or *The Never-Ending Story.*

Later on, we'd go see our cousins, who'd moved from Bogotá (Colombia) to Freehold (New Jersey), and frolic on their lawns and traipse through their adjacent woods. Our inner-city incredulity would fall away like a bad dream during these weekend visits. We'd run around like maniacs as soon as we got out of the rental car, which our parents procured for these weekend trips out to the land where there were no subways and everyone drove. The verdant suburbs were a release for us city kids. Even a single blade of grass—crisp, fibrous, organic—was exotic enough to prompt swift abandonment of the "New Yorker's prerogative," that mark of elitist cool that draws its yeast from bashing its western neighbor. All of a sudden, New Jersey wasn't so bad. Our cousins would take us exploring over railroad tracks, through abandoned lots, behind granaries and cornfields, skirting tracts of wooded parcels on old dirt roads whose caked-up mud tracks were engraved with wide diagonals of tractor tires. It all served to free us of our snobbery as we shed the dogmas of city life, the pride in a kind of Upton Sinclair blight, and embraced the exciting, more innocent Hardy Boys mystery we were apparently now on. (It was actually a murder mystery, as we came across a dead cat once. It was skinned from exposure, its jaw stretched out in a rictus of anguish. We concluded that it was no cat but the Jersey Devil itself. Case closed.)

Then, in our teens, the Hardy Boys saga gave way to a full-blown vision of Americana as my family moved to Lawrenceville, the township sandwiched between two of New Jersey's more famous cities, Princeton and Trenton. Like that tourism commercial, all of those visions of

America—the pristine roads, the yellow school buses, the sprinkler systems, the grassy soccer fields, the wide, open highways—had come to us through the lenses of commercial media, the opening credits of a sitcom, say, or the boilerplate family dramas of ABC Afterschool Specials. We understood them only as images. Yet here we were, expats of New York, on set, waiting to be picked up in the morning by the friendly neighborhood bus drivers who would always yell, "Hop on board!"—an extraordinary bit of familiarity compared to their counterparts at the MTA—after which we'd be driven to a high school with a parking lot surrounded by trees, with teachers who drank from coffee mugs and doors that opened to quiet hallways. This was the America that we'd always known about but that had been denied us in the city. It was like we were on TV. We felt like stars.

But I remember the looks my friends in Queens gave me when, after having moved, I came back to visit them and told them I now lived in New Jersey, how the corners of their mouths puckered into telltale smirks. I felt like I'd contracted something, a rash or a foul stench. And at least a part of me agreed with them. I felt guilty for "softening." I was now "one of them," a sellout, officially "B&T" (bridge and tunnel). "Do you live next to a toxic-waste dump?" I might've been asked, revealing the contradiction that lies within the popular imagination of New Jersey, that it is both paradise and hell, that it is at once a fake Eden of lawns and sprinkler systems and a dystopic garbage heap. The inconsistencies didn't register at the time, only the shame of betraying my urban provenance. But another part of me saw the light. This new setting, in its very fungibility as an American landscape, was secure in a way that New York never was, nor ever could be. The suburbs were like a trusted commodity. New York was (apparently) a broken system, but the suburbs were working. I didn't have to look over my shoulder all the time like I did in Elmhurst. Kids treated me differently because they knew I was from the city. I felt cool for the first time in my life. I was part of the suburban zeitgeist, no longer a denizen in the land of blight, where I was a misfit toy on a dangerous island, the gray, crime-ridden facade painted onto New York City by media; I was now a fresh-faced, suburban, so-called normal kid instead.

Was this true? How well founded were these feelings of relief after my family moved? Recalling a visit from a friend from New York seems to lend credence to these impressions. No sooner had he disembarked from the New Jersey Transit train than I could sense his enthusiasm. He was noticeably unaccompanied by the other, much-snottier friend who had rounded us out as a trio in Elmhurst, but he had a great time regardless. As we drove around at night and raced another car on a windy, remote road with the windows down, he exclaimed, referring to our missing compadre, "He doesn't know what he's missing!" It was a tear in the narrative fabric of the New Yorker's prerogative. It must've meant that the media depictions of suburbia that I grew up with were correct.

I was even beginning to wonder whether I'd ever even deserved to have this prerogative. Just how much of a Queens boy was I in the first place? I'd never developed a Queens dialect. Maybe that had to do with having immigrant parents, but I also think it resulted from the trouble I had fitting in in Queens. Perhaps I unconsciously rejected the neighborhood argot. I was never very tough or streetwise, nor was I the type, rampant among the working-class boys of Elmhurst in the '80s, to adopt any of those awkward, simian postures that preteen males put on to express their newfound lust for status and sexual adequacy. I was naturally intro-spective and sensitive in a way that was, frankly, a glaring liability. And I was punished for it, bullied constantly and dubbed the school geek. Con-sidering the trauma of grammar school, how tentative I was about these social rules, I think I would've had a difficult time as a young adult in Elm-hurst. It's hard for me to imagine finishing high school at the same time as having to navigate the complicated semiotics of the streets. I think I would've imploded.

Sometimes my story looks like a case study of the horrible practice of white flight. It gets complicated. There are many ifs in my family's move, many of which involve uncomfortable political and social implications. But it's important to understand that narratives about survival, which valorize traits like fortitude and cunning—what makes you "cool" to say you're from New York—never really had a chance to collide with the relief I felt when my family moved. Since I'd never felt that level of pride in the bootstrap culture of New York to begin with, since I'd never really bur-nished the New Yorker's prerogative, I had only the fear I felt living in the city to go off of. Interrogating the foundation of that fear is a life's proj-ect for me, but that doesn't take away the fact that I felt it all the same.

Seeing my friend from Queens here in Lawrenceville hooting out the open window as we were driving down the road at night, opting to waive his New Yorker's prerogative, if only for a night, was more than a vindica-tion. It was proof of being saved. You see, my friend happened to be fine in New York. Here in the suburbs, he was having fun, sure, but I couldn't imagine him actually living in New Jersey. Queens was his true home; that much was fact. Yet it was still possible for him to lose himself like this, to experience a liberty that the city mediated but that the suburbs did not. If it was true that, despite posturing about hardscrabble origins on the streets, the suburbs might melt away your defenses like this, then it meant that I'd stumbled onto good fortune with this move. It told me that I'd found a thing that would've proven elusive for me to hold onto in Queens.

New Jersey is a bit of a cipher, a story that still needs telling. This is what ties together various strains in the popular consciousness about the state—from *The Sopranos* to Springsteen—in a tangible, recognizable way. My contribution to that untold story, for better or for worse, is tied up with bodily freedom. This has created interpretative problems for me as an adult, given that privileges are what permitted that freedom in the first place. A lot of the confusion comes from the way the suburbs are pre-figured in the story America tells itself about itself: they have housed a middle-class success born of a different time in our history, and its images, through cinema, TV, and other media, have entered the deepest recesses of our personal narratives. Dogged tropes abound. Narratives about the suburbs as Edens needing protection from city vandals are unfortunately still prevalent.

But home is complicated regardless of the venue or the manner in which you find it and replicate it throughout your life. It is complicated even without the myths Americans have ascribed to the suburbs. And New Jersey is complicated, as befitting any state worthy of eulogy. It holds down the fort in the rhetorical battle between dueling prerogatives, the city one and the suburb one. I'll happily wrestle with all of this—maybe for the rest of my life—with what I might now joyously call my "New Jerseyan's prerogative."

New Jersey like You've Never Seen It

A Collection of Drone Photographs from Around the State

Manasquan pier. Photo by Kate Watt.

Castle ruins in Wanaque. Photo by Tim Kauger.

Rural Wantage. Photo by Brian Scully.

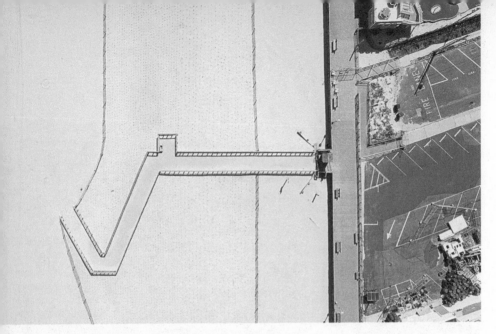

Point Pleasant Beach entrance. Photo by Jaclyn Sovern.

East Point Lighthouse, Heislerville. Photo by Donovan Myers.

Boardwalk plaza in Wildwood. Photo by R Justin McNeill.

Hamburg residential area. Photo by Dan Schenker.

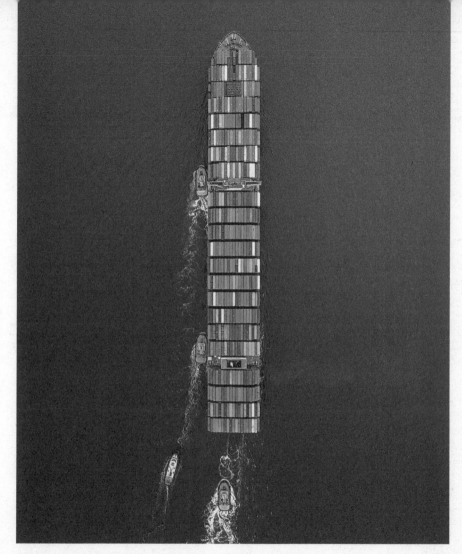

Cargo ship in Bayonne. Photo by Christopher Smith.

Miko Beach

A Couple of Blocks from the Boardwalk

MIKO BEACH

My grandmothers were from Puerto Rico, yet both ended up settling with their families in Jersey City, New Jersey. My father was a master painter and a "street hustler" of sorts, and before I was born, he was itching for a change of scenery. He packed up his family and moved us to South Jersey, to Ventnor City. My mother cried the whole ride here. She didn't know then that she would come to love this little island. My mother worked as a slot attendant for seventeen years at the Claridge Casino and was laid off on her birthday. I grew up with a lot of resentment toward the casinos. But I know my mom did the best she could. She worked a lot and yet still found time to take me to the beach almost every day of the summer. I spent weekends keeping my father company while he painted beautiful houses in Ventnor, Margate, and Longport. This is where I first fell in love with the smell of acrylic paint. I remember on days he didn't have to work, we would wake up at 4 a.m. to go fishing. We would bike all the way to our secret spot in Longport and watch the sunrise together. As I grew up, it was obvious how much I stood out among my peers. Spending so much time visiting family in Jersey City, my hometown, influenced me in every way: the music I listened to, the street art I was interested in, and even the clothes I wore. I felt so different from everyone else, and I wondered if my parents made the right decision to move. I craved the street culture of North Jersey and New York City, but I was stuck in a sun-bleached painting of the shore. I spent my early twenties angry, trying to escape. I lived in Tampa, then Jersey City, where I crossed the Hudson to explore New York City any opportunity I had. After a couple of years, I ended up back in the Ducktown neighborhood of Atlantic City with my father. I worked and focused on photography, working for numerous major brands over the years. At some point, my anger turned into gratitude for the blank canvas I call home. I spent the past decade watching this city be transformed by the local art community, and I'm honored to be a part of it all. 2020 brought me to my knees. It showed me what's most important: human connection and finding your community. I became so grateful I stayed in Atlantic City because I was present for my father's last days, which were thankfully filled with smiles and sunshine. A couple of months after he passed, I accidentally picked up a paintbrush again and began taking painting seriously for the first time in years. I created pieces that surprised me. It was almost as if my father was guiding me from beyond. I now recognize the blessing in each day spent a couple of blocks from the boardwalk with the ones I love.

Heaven in a Six-Hundred-Square-Foot Apartment

CAREN LISSNER

My little apartment at the top of the stairs had a broken ironing board that dropped out of the wall, old yellow linoleum floors, and a bathroom so narrow that I could sit on the toilet and rest my head on the opposite wall. Many of my roommates over the years—who were often starting their first job in Manhattan and wanted an inexpensive starter apartment across the river—loathed the place. But since I'd just spent two summers living in a car, that six-hundred-square-foot Hoboken walk-up was heaven to me. I think it saved my life.

I moved there after college during the early 1990s, seeking a publishing job in New York. I knew I couldn't afford to live in the Big Apple quite yet. I had $2,000 to my name, mostly from typing people's papers in school at the rate of a buck a page. I'd always heard, growing up in a quiet Jersey suburb, that New York was where you went to try to Be A Writer.

Hoboken offered lower rents than Manhattan, slightly larger apartments in long banks of brownstones, and a dollar-a-ride bus across the Hudson River. The city was popular enough with young people that when I went to a real estate agency, nothing was available. A recession had slowed new construction. On a cold December night, I walked around taping "Apartment Wanted" posters to poles throughout the mile-square city.

I got a call from a couple who was breaking up and leaving their two-bedroom. Their landlord said they could have their deposit back if someone assumed the lease. It was a "railroad apartment," meaning the rooms were one after the other, like train cars—so if I looked for a roommate to live in the smaller middle bedroom, I would have to traipse through it each time to get to the bathroom and kitchen. But the rent was only $800, and I knew I could find someone to split it.

"It has linoleum floors," the male half of the couple warned. "People don't like that because it's hard to clean. And it's a walk-up. No elevator." It sounded like he didn't want to leave. (I also got the impression he didn't want to break up.) But his loss was my gain. I paid the deposit and first month's rent—lucky for me, I got to avoid a realtor's fee—and I spent $30 of my remaining funds to place a roommate ad in the local weekly paper.

There was one problem: I promptly lost the mailbox key. Joe, my mustached mailman, knew I was broke and bravely yanked a bank of metal mailboxes out of the wall so I could take the lock to the locksmith, instead of paying them to come to me. The two of us saw an old letter fall out from behind the mailboxes. It bore a postmark from the 1980s. Joe said, "Wasn't my route back then," and we both laughed.

I would live in that apartment for the next fifteen years. It was a big change of pace from my childhood, during which I'd moved every year. Growing up, my brother and I would head to school, and my mom would sit in the dark and scour the *Asbury Park Press* classifieds for the one apartment or town that would finally make her happy. With each move, the rents got steeper, and we got poorer. She went through most of her savings but always wanted to find a new place, a new town. After I went off to college in Philadelphia, she often lived with my younger brother in a car. When I came home from college in summers, I slept in the backseat while she parked at supermarkets and minimalls. She was, at times, able to find cheap summer bungalows in dying resort towns like Buzzard's Bay, Massachusetts, or in the Catskills. Those times, I lay on dirty mattresses, the night air shooting at me from holes in the screens, and I dreamed about someday landing a steady job and apartment all my own.

After I moved into the walk-up in Hoboken after college, I had a succession of seven or eight roommates. They usually lived in the smaller room for six to nine months, then rotated out, vaulting toward adulthood. They either rented a place closer to their jobs in Manhattan or moved in with their college boyfriends. I was sometimes jealous of their apparent progress, but I was grateful to come home to the same apartment every day. I grew to love the place, with its ornate fleur-de-lis ceiling fixtures, a mysterious painted-over window between two bedrooms, and a set of keys all my own.

I never bought furniture because my roommates brought and left it: an antique wood bed frame, clocks, a green ironing board that wasn't broken. Sometimes my mom showed up and slept there for a few days, then drove back to the mountains to stay with my brother.

A few weeks after I moved into the apartment, I accepted a day job at the local weekly paper. I worked there by day, and each night, I'd sit beside my window overlooking Washington Street, revising my novels. Below me, hordes of people my age headed to the two Mexican restaurants that flanked my street, each offering fifty flavors of frozen margaritas.

I mailed drafts of three or four young-adult manuscripts to agents over the course of the 1990s, often getting typed letters back with basically the same message: "I don't think I can sell this, but please send me what you write next." Around the year 2000, I had the idea to write about a confused single girl who graduates from college and doesn't know how to fit in in New York City. The book was published when I turned thirty-two, during my tenth year in my little Hoboken apartment.

A few friends asked what I would spend the money on. While I gave some to my family and I bought a treadmill for exercise, I also gave myself the greatest gift I could: no more roommates. No more tiptoeing through someone else's room at night or worrying that I was typing too loudly. I could finally afford to have the place all to myself.

And during the holidays that year, instead of leaving Joe the usual $20 tip, I put $100 in an envelope with his name on it. I figured that after a decade delivering my rejection slips, he deserved a little of the success.

Block by Block

TEAM 1:1 NEW JERSEY

Many New Jerseyans capture and appreciate the glamour and charm of our home through painting, photography, and other visual media. In 2020, some members of Minecraft, a video game where you can build and explore whatever you like (restrained only by the fact that everything in the game is made out of blocks), began working on a massive feat: to re-create the entire Earth, 1:1 scale. Over one thousand members of Team 1:1 New Jersey is re-creating the entire state, from the welcoming beaches of Cape May on the Jersey shore to the peaks of the Appalachians in the chilly North.

We are building every single detail on every single building in every single area of New Jersey. Each bike rack, every sign, even every pothole that lies on our ever-so-deteriorating roads will be built to the best of our capability using the tools we are provided.

This is no easy task. Even with all the moderation and customization of the game, such as building tools and accurate teleportation, we are still limited by the technology of our time. Google Maps, our main source, does not have a perfect 3-D view or an updated eye-level view for every corner of the state. Yet, tenaciously, our builders pile on hard and undying work for the project. Some go on car rides to take pictures; some bike around their town to find the nooks and crannies that are not visible on Google. Team 1:1 New Jersey is committed to faithfully re-creating our wonderful state in Minecraft, no matter how long it takes.

Asbury Park

Montclair

East Rutherford

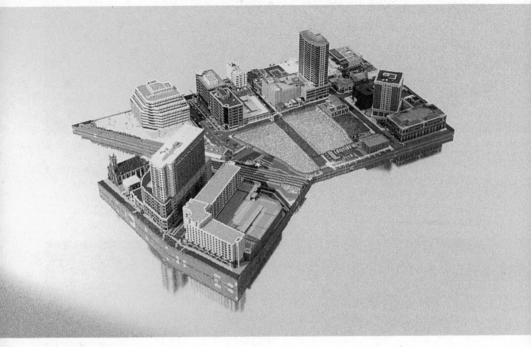

New Brunswick

Bagels, Bollywood, and Bhajans

RAAKHEE MIRCHANDANI

The ledger at Pooja International had little orange flowers on the cover. The same marigolds were printed on the glossy postcards of Hindu goddesses they sold at our local mandir. Each spread of the book was for a different customer, and the ruled lines were filled with Pooja Aunty's neat handwriting, a record of people who had come in, eager for the latest Bollywood releases she had somehow managed to score on VHS. The margins, separated by a thin, double red line, were the spaces for late fees.

"Good copy?" Mama would ask before we rented movies like *Tridev*, *Ram Lakhan*, or *Maine Pyaar Kiya*. Aunty would nod, though we all knew there were rarely good copies. But it was the early '90s, and these rows of videotapes were one of the few things my Desi mother and her American daughter had in common. They brought us to each other at a time we both felt like we belonged to no one.

For my mom, they were a connection to home she couldn't find anywhere else—not at Blockbuster and certainly not at ShopRite, where we took the long way around the store to escape the meat section. We were a couple of vegetarians who couldn't stomach the fish on ice with their bulging eyes or the live lobsters, claws banded together with thick blue rubber bands.

For me, the movies were a portal. Watching them was the first time I saw people who looked like us in the middle of a story, objects of desire and affection, beautiful, strong, funny characters who were the main draw, not a sideshow. And while I walked around cloaked in invisibility at school, in the bathroom at home, I'd practice Madhuri-style *thumkas* in the mirror, allowing myself to imagine what it felt like to be center stage.

On the way to the City, I often wondered what it would be like to stop on the lower level of the George Washington Bridge, the part where New York and New Jersey meet, to stick each leg in a different state. I thought about how I would answer, in that exact moment, someone who asked me where I was. Somewhere in between? Or not quite anywhere?

Walking the aisles at Pooja International, on Main Street in Hackensack, felt effortless, each item familiar and expected. Rows of favorites like Kurkure, Maggi noodles, Little Hearts, and boxes of Frooti filled the shelves. Okra, tindora, curry leaves, and little green mirchis overflowing in the produce section. We rarely got our pick of snacks or treats, but seeing that baby with a bowl cut, on the front of the Parle G packets, brought comfort in a way a trio of Keebler elves never could.

Our borders, if only here, were clear. And, of course, we never paid late fees.

My parents found themselves in Paramus by way of Flushing, Mumbai, Suriname, and the Philippines. They were a pair of Indian immigrants whose marriage was arranged on the Colaba streets where they grew up. Much of my childhood consisted of piecing together parts of India in New Jersey: Kathak class in Englewood, prayers at mandirs in Garfield, and potlucks in Paramus.

Most weekends we found ourselves in Closter, packed into the Sadhu Vaswani Center warbling religious songs in our mother tongue. The bhajans we learned were a far cry from the tunes we listened to on the ride over, packed in the station wagon. I'd perfected the skill of seamlessly switching from Ini Kamoze's "Hotstepper" to "Shukrana," from samosas to sandwiches. I was a girl with more hyphens than friends. My notebook said, "I love Adam Sandler," but the posters on my wall were Akshay Kumar, Aamir Khan, and Chandrachur Singh.

Indian American. First Generation. Asian American. Indo-Western.

But the Center, as we called it, was a place where we were just that: centered. Out of the margins, if even just for a couple hours a week. Tweens and teens, from various exits on the Turnpike, came together in a place that was built for us, by us. Kurtas and jeans, pizza after youth group, and the overwhelming comfort of not having to explain why our shoes were all piled up near the entrance.

I spoke Sindhi beautifully, wowing the uncles and aunties with my accent and vocabulary. I belted out the Hindu hymns, in front of hundreds, into the microphone. Fearless. I wrote essays and contributed to Bridge Builders, the Center's newsletter. I saw my name in print for the first time. Center stage, though in a slightly different way than I had dreamed.

I never once told anyone at school about any of it.

It's been nearly four decades since my parents rooted in the Garden

State. They don't know the difference between Bruce Springsteen and Bon Jovi—the only Boss they recognize is the Big B, Amitabh Bachan. But when you get them talking about bagels, it's undeniable: there's New Jersey in their veins now, too.

Bagels featured heavily in our family story. They still do. Flagels for my dad, cinnamon raisin for my mom. Pumpernickel for me, onion for my daughter and brother. We know every shop that makes them without eggs—vegetarians, can't take us anywhere—and will fight to the death about who makes the best ones. We often still break fluffy, seeded bread on the weekends, the invite that's almost always guaranteed to get everyone out of bed and together. My mother-in-law says bagels get stuck in her throat, but she's West Coast by way of Punjab. My aunt says they make her feel bloated, something about gluten and yeast. But she's not local either. I had to stop listening. It's a Jersey thing, and they just don't get it.

I've collected even more hyphens along the way since those years at the Center: working mother, writer-editor, caregiver and caretaker. Though there's one part of my identity that requires no hyphen, no oscillation.

Jersey Girl.

It's a seamless roll off the tongue, simultaneously an admission, invitation, and disclaimer, depending on what you need to know. I suppose in many ways, a Desi Girl is much like a Jersey Girl: brassy, spicy, and fiery. Magnetic. And together, Jersey Desi, a gutsy and gritty hyphen, the center of many orbits.

An Interview
with *Weird NJ*

BRANDON STOSUY

In the early '90s, Mark Sceurman started a newsletter featuring local news and weird history, legends, and folktales. A newspaper article in 1992 introduced it to people outside of Sceurman's friend group, so he stapled together the first three, creating issue number 1 of the beloved cult institution *Weird NJ*.

This was the heyday of zines. 1992 was also the year Nirvana's *Nevermind* reached number one on Billboard, and it felt like the underground was suddenly everywhere. As a punk teen growing up in the Pine Barrens—prime *Weird NJ* territory—I had my own zine, *whitebread*, which documented my life as a weirdo in a town of eight hundred. I'd send copies to other zine makers all the time. It was how I spoke to the world outside of Chatsworth, New Jersey, and it's how I made lifelong friends and collaborators.

This was true for Sceurman, too: one of the people who wrote to him for a copy of issue 1 was Mark Moran, who became Sceurman's collaborator

Mark Sceurman and Mark Moran of *Weird NJ*. Photo courtesy of WeirdNJ.com.

on the subsequent issues of the magazine as well as the book and television series to follow. They still do *Weird NJ* together over thirty years later.

As remote as I was, I knew about *Weird NJ* through other zines (like Jim Testa's *Jersey Beat*) and because it was eventually carried at Buzby's General Store, the only store within fifteen miles of my house. Having read (and lived) *Weird NJ* for so long, it was great to catch up with Sceurman, whom I'd never spoken to previously. We talked about the early days of the publication and how they led to the present.

How did you come up with the idea for *Weird NJ*, and how did you start doing it?

It was the early '90s, and I was immersed in the fanzine world. Everyone was doing photocopied publications about their favorite band or log cabins or whatever. I was trying to think of something else—I didn't want to do anything on music.

I thought, "How about something about New Jersey?" I thought more about it: "What about Weird New Jersey?" There was this book out then called *Weird America* that did similar things but not quite the same. It was all over the United States. I decided I was just going to do something about weird things in New Jersey. Think of a travel guide of things people might not want to see. That's really how it started. I didn't even know how to type. While I was learning, I said, "Oh, I'm just going to make a fanzine."

It was inspired by my love of local New Jersey history—old, weird history. Oh, this guy died on this spot or something. There's blood on the church pews at the church in Englishtown. That kind of thing.

The first issue was maybe fifty copies I sent around to my friends. Somebody from the *Bergen Record* got an issue, and that's when it really took off, because she did the interview with me, and all of a sudden I was getting a lot of letters. It was like, "Holy shit, how do I actually control this?"

This is how I met Mark [Moran]. He was very instrumental in partnering up with me and getting this thing off the ground. Because I was like, "Well, you know, this might work, it might not." But after six or seven issues, it's like, "Something's really happening here."

On weekends, we'd go to garbage dumps. Then we'd go to a semilocal legendary spot like Albino Village. Supposedly the Albinos will come out and kill you at night. After a while, I said, "Nobody's writing about this stuff. Nobody's looking at it as an oral history of the state. Nobody's written about Albino Village and Heartbeat Road and stuff like that."

I said, "This actually might be fun." I didn't think it would go past three issues, because it was just so ridiculous. I'm going to go to some junkyard one day, then we're going to go to a diner, then we're going to go see Albino Village, and now we're going to go see the Gates of Hell. But obviously it took off.

Have you ever worried about running out of weird places to go or running out of things to see?

You would think we would dry up after a while, but people keep sending ideas. They're like, "Well, you've got to go see this place. You've got to go see the Tomb of the Dead Nun," and things like that. It would snowball; it really did. This was before email and computers and stuff. So it would be hundreds of letters coming in. Everything had to be retyped and put in the zine.

But the beauty of New Jersey is that you can travel anywhere in three hours and be home for dinner. It's not like you're in Weird Colorado or anything. You can go anywhere within three hours and see desolation. You can see whole cities. You can see mountains. You can see anything you want. It's the perfect state to live in.

Also, these places don't last forever. And these sites, a lot of them burn down, a lot of them get vandalized. So we look at it as a history of the weird counterculture side of the state.

Are you still excited to do it?

What keeps it interesting is *Weird NJ* seems to be a conduit for every eccentric in the state that has a story to tell. We interview people that have sex with aliens. We interview people that believe they have a portal to the Inner Earth and it's in Tom's River. And these people really believe themselves. So we're not really judging anybody when we conduct interviews. They need a place to tell their story, and no one else is going to listen to them.

I think the newness of the magazine keeps it exciting. Whatever we discover in six months or wherever we travel, that's what we write about. And if a sidebar comes up that we have in our files, we'll throw that in there. It's really like a roll and tumble. There's no really set plan. We don't have any idea what the next issues are going to look like.

You started the magazine before social media. But now people can just hit you up on Twitter, they can find you on Facebook, all those kinds of things. How has that changed learning about weird places?

We do get a lot of emails about sites and everything, but the one true thing we still get are letters. We still get letters that you can tell these people don't have computers because they're writing it on index cards about some kind of alien that picked them up or whatever. Actually about two months ago, we got a handwritten letter with a bag of dirt in it that says, "This is dirt from Mars. I was one of colonization guys of Mars." And these guys, they're not faking it, believe me. We can tell a fake letter from a real letter. These guys are way out there. They're in their own alternative reality. So we just look at it and say, "Hey, that's a good letter. We'll print it."

Has anyone shown up at your house?

I had a couple of people drive by and take photos, never actually ring the doorbell. Sometimes it's a little scary. A lot of times people come up to me and say, "Well, what's the weirdest thing you've ever seen?" And I was like, "Well, it's not really the weirdest visual thing. It's like people we encounter are really strange."

There was this one place in Sussex County called the Profanity House. Whoever this kid was, he spent hours and hours in this abandoned house writing curse words all over the house. "Fuck your mother in the asshole." Something like that. And it was all over every inch of the house. I mean, who would do that? So you don't want to run into those people. Or there was one guy—this is a story sent into us—a guy was walking in the woods, and there was this guy dressed as an Indian tied to a tree. The guy goes, "Can I help you?" He goes, "No, leave me alone." So what the hell was going on there? [*Laughs*]

Everyone shares everything online. Has that made it harder to find complete mysteries? Growing up in Chatsworth, I had no internet until a certain point, and so no contact outside of getting the mail. That's not the case anymore. Are people beating you to the punch?

Well, to tell you the truth, we have hundreds of stories in the files. Like, some guy that's building a rocket blaster. He's going to shoot himself off in the backyard. So we have that in the files. He goes, "When I get my rocket ship ready, I'm going to call you guys, and I'm going to blast off in the backyard." A lot of times these letters don't even have return addresses. They want to keep it anonymous, but they want to tell their story. That's what we deal with. That's really how the magazine keeps on going.

Do you ever imagine being like, "I've reached my point. This is done." Or is this something that's become such a part of your life that you can imagine continuing to publish this for as long as you exist?

Mark and I sit at the office, and we say, "Well, you want to do another year?" "Well, what else are we doing?" We don't really work, you know; we just kind of edit and travel. You can do that until you die, I guess. As long as you got the money to print. That's the main drag on this whole thing is printing costs, mailing costs, and everything. It takes a big chunk out of a lot of the fun but is just the way it is. People say, "Well, if you're done with it, you don't want to do it anymore, why don't you just sell the business?" But I was like, "Well, the magazine is really an art project. It's not a magazine. It's our personalities. If we sell the business, what would it become?" It would become something boring and homogenized.

Do you have a team helping you, or are you really handling all aspects of the publication?

It's been Mark and I forever. We have Joanne Austin as an editor who looks out for all our mistakes and handles the social media. We answer every email that comes in. We answer every crackpot, everything. People have a personal connection with us. If someone doesn't get the right order in the mail, we call them up and say, "Sorry, we'll get it right this time." If they were getting *Martha Stewart Living*, Martha Stewart herself isn't going to call them up and say, "Sorry, I screwed up your order." So we keep it real. We keep it real, as New Jersey should be.

I do all the layout on the magazine. Mark does photography. We both do the writing. We have guest writers. We have a lot of submissions. Mark does a lot of the merchandise designs, like T-shirts and stickers and stuff. But that's it basically. . . . It only comes out two times a year. If it came out four times a year or if it came out six times a year, we would have given it up years ago. Because it's just too much. And really, you don't want a magazine called *Weird NJ* that comes out every month, because then that's when it gets saturated. That's when it wouldn't become fun anymore.

But *Weird* is nine to five, and after five o'clock, I devote my other half of the time to my other interests and family. I'm not *Weird* twenty-four hours a day.

Do you still think of *Weird NJ* as a zine?
Yeah. It's still done by the same two people; it just looks a little more professional because we have better printers and better graphic software. We still have the same typos, though. It's like a nightmare every time you send it out to press; it comes back, and it's like, "Oh, shit. Look at that typo on there." [*Laughs*] We like to think of it as homespun.

There's a little town square in Gillette that's home to an old church, a Mexican restaurant, and the remains of Archie's Resale Shop.

A former curiosities shop, museum, junkyard, and deer sanctuary,

the compound was run by local Santa impersonator

Archie Stiles.

My brother knows all about the local haunts.

Loved those days when Mom would take us for a nature walk, enchiladas, and a trip to Archie's.

Lives in LA now

Sigh. I miss summer breaks.

Remember the doll room? Or the one just, like, full of prosthetics?

Yeah, wild. I wonder what happened to all of that stuff after he died. And what about the deer?!

I miss the lost local lore of my youth.

179

The two of us have always been drawn to the places that didn't fit easily into the suburban structure.

Remember when those retro pastel houses were suddenly bulldozed at the Nike Missile Base on Route 10?

How many times did you explore the abandoned wings of Greystone at night?

The things that felt unusual, untold, and uncomfortable... like growing up Black in Morris County.

But that's for another call.

WT

Why I Left

ALICIA COOK

I spent a long stretch of my life in the same town that many people only visit during the summer. I went to school here, grew up with my siblings here, had my first kiss here, was in my first (and second) car accident here, fell in love here, had my heart broken here, landed my first job here, got married here. You get the gist. I *lived* here; my being is *ingrained* here, which is entirely different than visiting here. When you spend years of your life, your most formidable years at that, where others only vacation, you walk away with a different type of sand in your eye.

I often dreamed of escaping *from* the same place others looked forward to escaping *to*. Choices and mistakes and other life moments piled up and obstructed sunset views and my perception of what this town really meant to me. Over the years, I developed a problematic relationship with my hometown, which very well may double as your "home away from home."

I have had to say good-bye to friends in the funeral home directly across the street from every tourist's favorite ice cream parlor. The lines were always equally as long, and I never appreciated the rigid dichotomy between us and them. I lost my virginity, and a number of car keys, to the same waves that panicked beachgoers were always pulling their chairs away from. I never understood why they would set up their beach camp that way. I always saw the tide coming.

It grew difficult to maintain my balance here. I started to stumble over my own roots because my hometown remembered too much. I was here before and after the hurricanes, both Sandy and the lonely one that ravaged above only my head. I have been the happiest and the saddest here.

I have always liked how the air smelled here after a late-August downpour and how our dogs barked at passing boats the way land-loving canines did the mailman. I always considered Local Summer the fifth season of the year. I always liked the way freshly fallen snow looked next to sea foam. I always liked catching crabs, celebrating Halloween on October 30 and Easter on the boardwalk, and having sand on the floor of my car year-round. And, maybe more than anything, I liked how the ocean restored my peace of mind.

For the majority of my life, no matter how upset or confused I was, I could sit by the ocean and actually feel my body and mind click back into a more positive space. Then, one day, the ocean couldn't fix me anymore. It was like its magic had worn off. Once my sacred refuge, it just reminded me of the bad times.

I began to avoid the Atlantic Ocean like some people do mirrors. Sometimes when I was near the ocean, I cringed the way I do when I find an old journal. I didn't want to face who I was or what I had been through. The ocean knew that person and all her secrets. The ocean would never let me forget that person, and reminders constantly washed up to my feet with the sea glass and pebbles.

If you're lucky to live long enough, you learn that you can spend too much time in one place. What used to recharge you begins to drain you. What used to bring you peace begins to haunt. Your safe haven becomes a crime scene. I couldn't stand behind the yellow tape anymore with a forced smile on my face, so I left.

I didn't run away, but I also didn't look in my rearview as I hopped on Garden State Parkway North. I didn't wield a match or leave a trail of gasoline behind me. I left gracefully and with a "see you soon," so I would never have to leave for good. I *wanted* to come back. I *wanted* to love the ocean again. In order to repair my relationship with this town, I had to leave.

The writer Terry Pratchett once said, "Why do you go away? So that you can come back. So that you can see the place you came from with new eyes and extra colors. And the people there see you differently, too. Coming back to where you started is not the same as never leaving."

If I had stayed, my resentment might have become irreversible. Distance helped me regain perspective. Now, I return to my hometown with appreciation and gratitude in my heart. When I visit with my old town, I look forward to grabbing a coffee from Rook on my way in, and I'm reminded that many good things happened here. I don't white-knuckle my steering wheel anymore as I drive down Route 35. My parents are happy to see me here again, and I am happy to not have to use my GPS for a few days. I meet up with the ocean like I do an old friend who knows everything about me but still loves me anyway.

I am no longer jaded; I can see why so many people flock to these shores each summer. Because this place *does* hold magic, but you can only conjure it if you believe in it enough.

I believe again.

A History of New Jersey, in Artifacts

BRITTNEY INGERSOLL

New Jersey's wealth of historical institutions scattered throughout the state work to preserve and share different aspects of our state's history. The institutions included here are of various historical scopes and consist of museums, historical societies, and libraries. They are essential spaces of knowledge that preserve items of the past for today and for generations to come. The variety of these objects—examples of political, social, entertainment, and science history—truly signifies the multifaceted history of New Jersey.

Battleship *New Jersey*. Battleship *New Jersey* (BB-62) was commissioned at the Philadelphia Naval Shipyard in 1943 and completed four assignments before being preserved as a museum on the Camden, New Jersey, waterfront in 2001. She is seen here with her crew manning the rails while entering Pearl Harbor during her fourth commission in the 1980s. Official US Navy photo from the Battleship New Jersey Museum and Memorial collection.

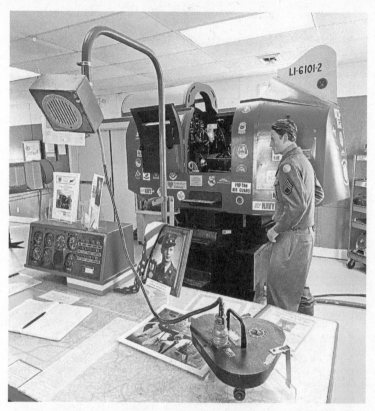

Link Trainer. The Link Trainer, also known as the "Blue Box," was the premier instrument used for safe flight instruction during World War II. It looks like a small wooden airplane cockpit, with an instrument panel lined from top to bottom with dials and gauges used for determining altitude, fuel levels, and manifold pressure. This one is one of just five in the entire world that are operational. Photo courtesy of the Millville Army Air Field Museum.

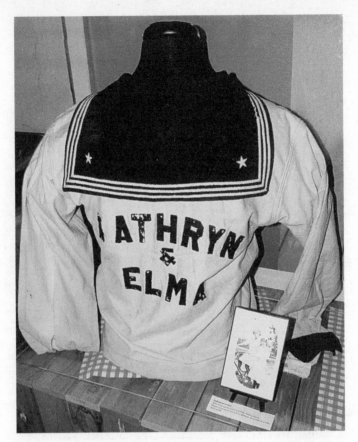

Race costume from the schooner _Kathryn and Elma_. This race costume was worn by the crew of the schooner _Kathryn and Elma_ during the one-time Great Delaware Bay Schooner Race of August 1929. The lavish race was the pinnacle of the oystermen's wealth and excess, which came to a crash six weeks later at the start of the Great Depression. Photo courtesy of the Bayshore Center at Bivalve/Delaware Bay Museum.

Clovis projectile point. This stone spear point, called a Clovis point, was fashioned around 11500 to 8000 BC and used by some of the earliest people to live in present-day New Jersey. The Native Americans who fashioned this tool lived a nomadic lifestyle during the Ice Age. Spear points like this were used to hunt big game such as mammoth and mastodon. From the collection of the Alan Ewing Carman Museum of Prehistory in Cumberland County.

The Pageant of the Paterson Strike program cover. In January and February 1913, more than twenty-four thousand men, women, and children marched out of the silk mills of Paterson, New Jersey, calling for decent working conditions, an end to child labor, and an eight-hour workday. The home of Pietro and Maria Botto in neighboring Haledon, New Jersey, served as a haven for free speech and assembly for immigrant workers of many nationalities. On June 7, 1913, the Pageant, a fund-raising event that reenacted the strike, was performed at Madison Square Garden. The program cover was designed by Robert Edmund Jones. Courtesy of the American Labor Museum/Botto House National Landmark.

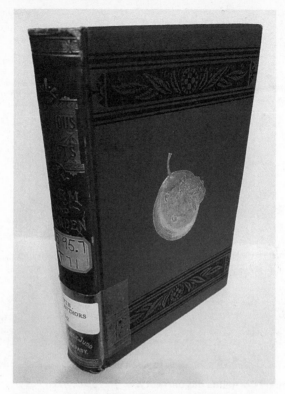

***Injurious Insects of the Farm and Garden* by Mary Davis Treat.** Mary Davis Treat, a naturalist, corresponded with Charles Darwin and other well-known nineteenth-century scientists and authored a number of books based on her research. One, titled *Injurious Insects of the Farm and Garden*, was so popular that it was reprinted five times. Photo courtesy of the Vineland Historical and Antiquarian Society.

Robert Cornelius daguerreotype. This photograph was taken by Robert Cornelius, known for opening the first photograph studio in Philadelphia (only second in the United States) and for taking the first photographic self-portrait (or "selfie") on May 26, 1840. The image was taken in Cornelius's first studio and is one of the earliest photographs in US history. A notation on the back of the photograph reads, "first daguerreotype that came to Salem, NJ. May 26, 1840." From the collection of the Salem County Historical Society.

Jug and crock. Utilitarian and spare in function and form, these vessels are made of stoneware. The Garden State was one of the earliest centers for stoneware production and yielded some of the best clay deposits, creating a thriving market crucial to the state's economy and labor market. More traditional in design with less figural and floral decoration, this jug and crock incorporate flourishing script in cobalt slip of two local businesses: Stiner Bros., a Madison, New Jersey, grocery store, and W. H. Meslar, a Morristown, New Jersey, general store. These vessels give further insight into community exchange, local industry, and domestic preservation in Morris County, New Jersey, in the nineteenth century. Photo courtesy of the Museum of Early Trades and Crafts.

FRANK SINATRA

October 3, 1990

Dear Terry and Friends at the Hoboken Public Library,

We had a microcosm of the world in Hoboken...
immigrants from all over brought their traditions,
languages, foods. I remember coming home from
school, or a friends house or just hanging around,
and smelling all the wonderful aromas coming from
each tenement apartment. I have marvelous memories
of that town and I applaud you all for keeping it
special

Wherever I've traveled these many years, I often
think back to the days growing up in Hoboken.
Watching the trains go by, jumping on the ferry
to Manhattan, singing on a table in my father's
tavern, daydreaming in class at Demerest High,
getting into trouble on the docks...they were pretty
exciting times.

Congratulations on 100 years of being there, Hoboken
Public Library. I may not have spent much time in
the building on Park Avenue, but we are all family.

With much love,

Frank Sinatra

Ms. Terry Sasso
Hoboken Public Library
500 Park Avenue
Hoboken, New Jersey 07030

Letter from Frank Sinatra to the Hoboken Public Library.

The singer and actor Frank Sinatra was born in Hoboken, New Jersey, on December 12, 1915. On October 3, 1990, Sinatra sent a letter, recounting some of his recollections of growing up in the city, to the Hoboken Public Library's former director Terry Sasso, in regard to the Hoboken Public Library's one hundredth anniversary. Courtesy of the Hoboken Public Library.

Going Home to New Jersey

CAITI BORRUSO

Once you've been doing it long enough, you learn not to aim for a specific train, especially not on a Friday night out of Penn, and instead to rocket yourself from the A once it gets to 34th, to check the big red and white letters of the board, and to punch, without thinking, the shoddy screens for your pink ticket. And you know where there are outlets scattered, you know the pigeon inside the Amtrak waiting room, where sometimes they let you sit and sometimes they don't, and the days that bookend holiday weekends often have military members with rifles. Mostly it is a smooth motion from one train to the other; usually there is a train waiting or one about to be waiting, disappearing from the last bits of sun in Secaucus and emerging in the dark in midtown, where then, wearily, the floodgates will open, and all the commuters move in one solid thrumming mass to claim seats.

When I was a child, the blue fish-scaled seats and pink walls of the NJ Transit trains were our link to New York, to what we considered then as

Photos by Caiti Borruso

culture: the myriad of options offered at Madison Square Garden, Times Square, the American Museum of Natural History. On Wednesdays as a kid, when my dad had custody of us, he showed us how to place pennies on the rails and retrieve them after the trains passed. On weekends, there was a shoddy flea market in one of the parking lots, and parking was free in the other. In high school, the trains ferried me to bad concerts, to college visits, and to my mother's cancer treatment. The first time I took the train alone to New York was to see her, sometime during the spring of my senior year of high school, after a surgery that required an overnight stay. I knew the perforated mauve slips of NJ Transit tickets but had no idea how to use the subway, so I walked the twenty-something blocks over to her.

Once in college, I lived an hour's subway ride from Penn Station; I took the G to the A or the C, depending on which showed up first, and then it was an hour and twelve minutes or so to Aberdeen-Matawan. Once my train passed Perth Amboy, I could reliably call my mother, who would be at the station waiting in the car for me. Once the train passed one specific spread of shaggy marsh grass, I could reliably gather my things and stand in the vestibule waiting, watching my reflection flicker in and out. I always had at least three bags: one for clothes, one camera bag, and one long, awkward tripod bag. It was usually dark, because it was either the fall or the winter or the early spring; and the puppy she adopted at the beginning of my sophomore year was usually in her lap, and she was usually smoking a cigarette and would kiss the side of my face before driving the five minutes back to our house.

The very first time I made the trip home from New York, the escalator down to the platform broke, and we all tumbled down its steps. I fell onto the prongs that help glide people downward. My carpetbag—absolutely impractical, bulky and green and floral, purchased at Goodwill months earlier—went before me, and the man behind me on the steps put his hands under my armpits and righted me. It was as if nothing had happened. On the train, I inspected the damage: two small holes in my pant legs and two trickles of blood; I still have two vertical scars, one on each shin.

In college, and after, the train was a familiar space, one where I was nearly always alone, my knees drawn up onto the seat in front of me, the wide plate window expansive next to me. Taking the train felt like it belonged to a different place than New Jersey and a different time; I felt like a girl in Europe, someone in a movie; but the window was sticky with someone else's forehead oil, and I was still me. I used my ticket as a book-mark until the conductor came to take it; and all my things were stacked beneath my legs, and sometimes I would take out whatever camera I had and make a picture. The train rambled along through Newark and Eliz-abeth, across the marshes that resembled my own neighborhood, past empty factories and across one wide swath of bay. Eventually it would glide past my aunt's former home, which overlooked the water and the tracks, and then the electricity would briefly drop, due to a change in voltage; and the whole train would go dark and quiet, and we would all hold our breath. Or I would, and I would look up, unable to read my book if it were winter still, until we had passed under the bridge. When my best friend lost her grandmother one April and her uncle the next and her father the year after, I took the train in for each funeral and back out; we both descended on the town, met outside the church where my parents had married, drank at the bar in the basement of the fire station.

When my mother sold my childhood home, I went back for one last weekend, to finish packing up my things, to do one final subway–Penn Station–NJ Transit loop. That Friday morning, an Amtrak train derailed at Penn, suspending all trains out of the city. My mother suggested an Uber or a bus, neither of which seemed right. It was early, I had happened to check the news, and I turned to my boss and told him I had to go. I walked a long way to the J train in my yellow rain coat and then walked a long way to the ferry dock in lower Manhattan. It was my father's preferred method into the city, but I had never taken it before; it was too expensive, it was too slow, it wasn't the train. It was a long wait in drizzle on the dock, and when the time came, I sat inside with my bags at my feet. The Verrazzano Bridge loomed above, sweet blue against gray sky, and as we sailed beneath it, my belly swooped. "This will be healing, I think," I had told my mother over the phone as I waited. I didn't know when to call my grandpa to tell him to be waiting for me at the dock, and so he was very early, in the cold of March's spring. Later that night, the ferry would beach itself in the Highlands, and I would write, "It was a bad day for people going home to New Jersey."

The LGBTQ Community's Complicated Relationship with New Jersey

Written by Sarah Prager
Illustrated by Veronica Casson

LGBTQ+ people have an incredibly complex relationship with New Jersey that involves a push and pull (particularly with neighboring New York City) that has been unfolding for centuries. While the Garden State has been at the forefront of LGBTQ+ rights compared to other U.S. states throughout the 21st century, few of the famous LGBTQ+ Americans born in New Jersey stayed there. From precolonial through modern times, New Jersey's LGBTQ+ history is anything but simple.

Precolonial and Colonial Times

Like in most of the Americas before the arrival of Europeans, the indigenous peoples of what is now New Jersey had different ideas around gender, sex, and sexuality than the invading colonizers. In dozens of tribes—some scholars say most tribes—there were three or more genders.

Once New Jersey was a colonial province, "sodomy" and "buggery" were made capital offenses at the very first meeting of the assembly in 1668. After the American Revolutionary War, the state of New Jersey changed its law in 1796 to make sodomy no longer punishable by death, but by a fine and up to 21 years of solitary imprisonment with hard labor. It was one of the first states to do away with the death penalty for sodomy.

After years of softening the law, New Jersey repealed its anti-sodomy law entirely in 1978, long before the 2003 Supreme Court ruling that nullified all remaining anti-sodomy state laws in the United States.

Leaving for Queerer Pastures

Some of the United States' most prominent and historically significant LGBTQ+ leaders have come from New Jersey, but almost none of them stayed there.

Marsha P. Johnson (1945–1992) was born in Elizabeth before leaving for Greenwich Village as soon as she graduated high school. She went on to become an important gay liberation and trans rights activist.

Barney Frank (born 1940) is now most associated with Massachusetts since he represented the commonwealth from 1981 to 2013 in Congress, but he was born and raised in Bayonne before attending Harvard. In 1987, he became the first member of Congress to come out as gay voluntarily.

Pop star Halsey (née Ashley Frangipane 1994) was born in Edison and told Nylon Magazine in 2014, "I grew up in New Jersey, and I would always take the train into New York, and I was getting into a lot of trouble. When I was 17 I was seeing a guy who was 24 and he lived on Halsey Street in Brooklyn. That's where I first starting writing music and where I started to feel like I was a part of something bigger than my town in middle of nowhere New Jersey."

Darren Young (born 1983) was the first professional wrestler to come out as gay while still signed to the WWE. He was born and raised in Union and attended Fairleigh Dickinson University in New Jersey before pursuing his wrestling career.

Did all of these LGBTQ+ people of note leave because they felt like New Jersey was the "middle of nowhere"? For many, they were likely drawn to the energy and community of the largest queer hubs in the world or wanted to leave unsupportive family behind.

A Queer Life of Its Own

That's not to say they couldn't have found any queer culture in New Jersey. In 2016, graduate students from Rutgers-Newark wrote for NOTCHES about Newark's ballroom scene that has been around since the 1980s: "Newark, New Jersey's LGBTQ+ community does not receive the same focus as those in major cities such as NYC or San Francisco. Yet, our city has a dynamic queer scene with fascinating historic roots."

New Jersey has its own queer life, as the stories from the Queer Newark Oral History Project capture. One of the earliest recorded queer people living in Newark was a 21-year-old who was arrested in 1885 who the police called a "make believe masculine," someone who "passed at her boarding house as a boy."

The 2003 murder of Sakia Gunn, a Black butch lesbian who was stabbed to death at the age of 15 after she turned down two men at a bus stop in downtown Newark, mobilized the local queer community. An estimated 2,500 people attended Gunn's funeral.

Timothy Stewart-Winter and Whitney Strub wrote for OutHistory.org that "community could be found in nearby New York, but also locally, albeit in ways that were always mediated by Newark's fraught history of racial tensions and segregation. As a working-class city with an African American majority since 1965, Newark's queer history departs from the more familiar narratives of New York, Philadelphia, Los Angeles, or San Francisco, where white-led activist groups loom large in the historical writing."

New Jersey as Homestead Destination

While many queer people born in New Jersey didn't stay, many who weren't born there sought it out and found a quiet home there as an escape from the busy city. Whether for weekends at the beach or a retirement on a farm, the natural landscape of New Jersey drew New Yorkers and others.

Poet Walt Whitman (1819-1892) wrote part of *Leaves of Grass* at Laurel Springs in southern New Jersey where he spent much of his time from 1876 to 1884. He lived out his final days in Camden in a house now open to the public as the Walt Whitman House (near the Whitman Woods and the Walt Whitman Bridge and so on). He called Laurel Lake in Camden County the "most beautiful lake."

Dr. Sara Josephine Baker (1873-1945) was also drawn to nature in New Jersey. After a life in the most densely populated parts of New York City working on public health, Baker moved in the 1930s with her life partner, Ida Wylie, to a farm in Princeton, where they lived with a third woman, Dr. Louise Hansen. The three were known locally as "The Girls," and Wylie wrote in her autobiography that they lived "amicably and even gaily together."

The natural beauty of New Jersey offered a peacefulness that New York City could not, and so the two places seemed to trade queer historical figures back and forth over the last two centuries, some seeking a big city and others looking to leave it.

A Modern Leader

New Jersey repealed anti-sodomy laws and legalized same-sex marriage before federal decisions did so nationally. Though federal laws have not been passed criminalizing conversion therapy or requiring LGBTQ+ history to be taught in schools, New Jersey was the second state to pass laws to both of those effects. As a national leader consistently ahead of the curve, New Jersey is a legislatively welcoming place in the 21st century, with anti-discrimination laws in place for both sexual orientation and gender identity.

While a looming neighbor gets a lot of national attention, New Jersey is a beacon of queer life in its own right.

Illustration by Elise Sacco

Fable and Flora

The Home of the Jersey Devil

ELISE SACCO

The Pine Barrens have a generational affiliation with the Jersey Devil. The legend is so prolific among people living in the region that it seems that bodies raised on their sandy soils have a muscle memory for seeking out the storied creature. At dusk, ears anticipate the click of cloven hooves on metal roofs or an unearthly cry from an unseen entity. Even when driving down the Parkway, many people find their peripheral vision compulsively fixed on the tree line for a glimpse of enormous bat wings unfolding between the pitch pines. For centuries, the 1.1-million-acre landscape has served as a backdrop for a cryptid to inhabit; however, perhaps the most devilish aspect of the Pine Barrens isn't a winged quadruped at all.

Early European settlers described the region as a hell on Earth, a lush, inviting forest that yielded acidic, nutrient-poor soil unfit for cultivating even the most undemanding crops. The only water to be found was tannin-tinted creeks whose iron deposits could make smaller streams run as red and thick as blood. Desolate stretches of white sand heathlands surrendered to impossibly thick forests that swallowed man-made paths overnight. Those who were lost in the woods rarely returned, succumbing to bitter cold or sugar sand pits. And, most disturbingly, settlers found that frequent wildfires seemed not only tolerable but essential to the life cycle of the cursed forest. Fires hot enough to obliterate every living organism swept through often, disintegrating underbrush and destroying human settlements. But the Barrens could endure the unendurable, and just days later, neon-green shoots would sprout out of the charred bark of blackened pitch pines. For centuries, this infernal life cycle has been fighting against human influence and galvanizing an ecosystem that is absolutely unique to the known world. As the rest of New Jersey's wilderness withdrew like the curled edges of a burned page, the inhospitable Pine Barrens became a haven for all that was rare and special, both in folklore and in biology.

The modern Pine Barrens have been shaped and maintained by fire. In hearing this, you would think that the ecosystem has adapted to withstand a fire-prone area, perhaps by maturing into a low-flammability environment or creating wetter conditions. However, the opposite is true; if anything, the Barrens have evolved to be incendiary by nature. Because of the high soil acidity, no bacteria linger to decompose brush that falls to the forest floor. This leads to an extremely dry, dense blanket of pine needles, leaves, and natural litter that could ignite with a single errant ember. The sandy, nutrient-poor soil has a low water-holding capacity, leading to even drier conditions. Thirty percent of the ground is occupied by highly flammable pitch pines, whose community survival depends on frequent wildfires. Without fire clearing the underbrush, pine seedlings cannot penetrate to the forest floor and proliferate into saplings. Also, while pitch pines dominate the Pine Barrens, they can only do so if oaks and other hardwood trees are naturally culled by wildfire. Without frequent fires, pitch pines would be strangled by oak trees that grow taller and wider, blocking out sunlight and competing for moisture and minerals. With dense, resinous bark, pitch pines can withstand an inferno that hardwood trees cannot. And, most miraculously, the Barrens' pitch pines have evolved to grow serotinous cones, which lay dormant and will not bud unless exposed to intense heat. After a wildfire, these buds will awaken and grow through the hook-shaped basal crooks of scorched pitch pines. Sometimes biology is more awe-inspiring than legend; walking through a steaming forest and seeing radiant-green sprouts growing through charred bark can make one feel like they've stumbled out of reality. It's easy to see why European settlers saw this forest as something harrowing and ancient, a place where only the devil could live.

While the Pine Barrens have shown no endearment to humanity, the acidic soil and water conditions have turned the forest and surrounding lowlands into a dwarf planet for the most curious organisms New Jersey has to offer. Because carnivorous plants like sundews and bladderwort don't require wet or nutritious soil, they grow freely. After a rainfall, it's not uncommon to see swollen pitcher plants digesting spiders, small animals, or moths. Alongside predatory plants, even rarer ones grow. Wild orchids that usually require wet, nutrient-rich soil somehow thrive in the Pine Barrens, adding to their extraterrestrial landscape. Wetland wildflowers that have been virtually decimated in every other corner of the world have found safe haven in the heathlands. Bog asphodel, named from the

Latin word for "bone breaker," is thought to survive solely in the New Jersey Pine Barrens. Additionally, incidences of the Pine Barrens gentian and swamp pink are dwindling outside of New Jersey. Globally rare moth species also thrive in the lowlands, and some are unique to this area alone—the only known occurrence of the Daeke's pyralid moth occurred in the Pine Barrens.

In addition to harboring nearly 130 endangered or threatened species, the harsh landscape has resulted in many organisms making peculiar adaptions. The heath family of plants that occupy the forest understory have evolved to prosper in acidic soil; how these species handle these conditions is not yet understood. The surface waters of the Pine Barrens average a 4.4 pH level, acidic enough to dissolve a human tooth. Most fish and amphibians are unable to tolerate a pH below 6, but creatures such as the Pine Barrens tree frog and pickerels have adapted to reproduce and thrive in acidic conditions. What was once thought to be a barren stretch of wilderness is home to an otherworldly group of organisms that have not only survived but also blossomed in a monstrous environment. They inhabit the uninhabitable. When we know this, a centuries-old cryptid stalking the forest doesn't seem like such a stretch of the imagination.

Sitting in the comfort of my home, it's easy to write about why an environment that makes no concessions to humanity makes a perfect home for the Devil. But when you are in the center of the Pine Barrens, lush and green and alive, it's impossible to pull back and see their entirety. It is steel wrapped in silk: on its surface, it is a welcome stretch of desolation constructed of sphagnum moss and tea-colored streams. But at its heart, this land is a singular organism. Just as the Leeds Devil devoured the midwife, the sugar sand pits of the Barrens can shift under unsuspecting feet and swallow visitors whole. White cedar forests filter and absorb pollutants like kidneys, preventing man-made toxins from poisoning the body. Between the ribs of pitch pine roots, sandy soil lies over the water table as thinly as a blood vessel, allowing rainwater to filter through. But, like a body, the formidable Pine Barrens have a fatal softness; the same earth capable of devouring a man whole also drinks agricultural runoff, highway rock salt, and sewage disposal. Increased development of the areas surrounding the pines have led to decreased water quality, invasive species, and fire suppression.

The Original People, known as the Lenni-Lenape tribe, understood that prescribed burns were essential to the health and rebirth of the forest they inhabited. While modern prescribed burning was implemented by the New Jersey Department of Environmental Protection in many areas of the Pine Barrens starting in 1948, increased demand for fire suppression by surrounding communities threatens to interrupt the essential fire cycle that maintains the distinctive ecosystem. Oak trees, while beautiful, are a threatening malignancy to the Barrens as they exist today; if they are allowed to grow freely, pitch pines and all of the organisms they support will fade away. Many of the endangered species that the Barrens protect do not exist in well-established communities anywhere else in the world. Once they are gone from the Pine Barrens, they will probably disappear forever. Untouched land is a precious commodity all on its own in modern times, but the loss of such a unique and ancient environment would be devastating. Humankind is naturally protective of and awed by mythical legends like the Jersey Devil but is willing to destroy a diverse ecosystem that is every bit as rare, magical, and monstrous.

The Pine Barrens, like the famous Devil it houses, have endured centuries of changes, misconceptions, and human influence. It is remarkable in its wildness, its diversity, and its absolute defiance to the modern world. While you may be inspired to visit in hopes of glimpsing a mysterious creature, I hope you can appreciate that the ecosystem is a living beast all on its own. But, unlike the Jersey Devil, the Pine Barrens are indisputably real. The most harrowing part of New Jersey's dearest legend may not be the storied beast at all but the tangible and extraordinary place it inhabits.

Alone on the Turnpike

LUCY DEAN STOCKTON

You crashed my Honda Civic on a hill in the Philadelphia suburbs immediately after boasting of your parking prowess. You clearly live without the same fearful hesitancy that I do—but let it be known that while I passed my driver's test at seventeen by smiling at my instructor and promising I'd learn how to parallel park, I would never have such hubris today. Unlike you, who push fearlessly through your limits, I have always honored mine. I wanted to look for parking somewhere a little less steep, to drive a few blocks away and walk, given that I cheated my way into a driver's license and never did learn to maneuver my car backward. But it was with that confidence that you accidentally accelerated into the parked car in front of mine, grimacing when the metal squealed. It was my task to salvage the weekend, assuaging your guilt, running my fingers through your soft blond curls, and insisting, "This is what car insurance is for, babe." I drove back to New York on Sunday, never accelerating past fifty, with a broken headlight and an eviscerated fender, the metal contorted like modern art.

I, alone, met the eyes of fellow drivers on the New Jersey Turnpike who laughed at the metal hanging off my car and fluttering over the superhighway in the gray sleet and wind. I fixed the bumper days later, but it would take years to disentangle myself from the wreckage of our breakup.

I-95 was built throughout the 1950s as part of a special project to connect the eastern seaboard North to South, from Maine to Florida. I grew up in the backseat on this continental superhighway, traveling south to Pennsylvania and Washington, DC, or north toward Boston and Maine, through New York, stopping always in the miraculous impossibility that is Queens, where my family is from. The New Jersey section of I-95, colloquially termed "the Turnpike," was, in most regards, the only way in which I saw the state. New Jersey was an afterthought destination-wise, aside from a few trips to the Jersey Shore or the hugely anticipated but equally dreaded amusement park visit. And among New Yorkers with a superiority complex, my fourth-generation Queens family included, the state was derided as a pale imitation of New York, offering its own versions of greenery, shorelines, and comparatively diminutive city skyline. New Jersey is a state defined and erased by its superhighway.

But the Turnpike *is* a noteworthy and singular feat built among oil tankers, power lines, and rusting crosshatch bridges on top of a vast, coastal wetland. It is hard to overstate the anthropogenic nonhumanness of it: something that industrialists could only dream of, with almost zero attention toward aesthetic, long stretches of highway soaring over bypasses, punctuated by crumbling exits and tightly wound off-ramps spiraling out of view. If you believe that industrialists had the right idea, it's a tremendous human accomplishment—but if the veil is lifted on the limitations of profit-driven manufacturing triumph, the Turnpike reveals itself as a dystopian, crumbling concrete infrastructure. As you're ushered between mile markers or transported between dotted lanes, heading from metropolis toward metropolis, crowded between careening metal infrastructure, you are no one among strangers.

Driving from Philadelphia to New York, stewing in an everlasting breakup, this anonymity was bliss to me. And I was definitely not alone. In 2017, the Turnpike had four hundred million unique transactions; the vast majority of them were people commuting to said metropolises or taking weekend trips. A microscopic portion of this leisure-oriented subgroup were twenty-something girls desperately clinging to their ex-girlfriends. It was comforting to abandon my camp in favor of the commuters, joining the millions of people with different lives speeding toward something. As another anonymous body in a standard-issue car, I could forget myself, and I wondered if this was the transformation I was promised.

In the United States, the car is the promise. Maybe best expressed by Herbert Hoover's 1928 presidential campaign slogan, "a chicken in every pot and a car in every garage," driving culture is an integral part of our national ethos. Cars are so central to the American interpretation of independence, mediated through the language of convenience and autonomy, that they are often a material symbol of its more elusive value: freedom. Driving on superhighways reflects that value (despite the fact that people drive on mutually cooperative, publicly funded roads), allowing people to self-segregate, maintaining a facade of autonomy in an isolated, insulated metal cocoon.

The pseudoprivate space of the car, articulated by the sociologist Deborah Lupton, creates a sociological "cyborg experience" (itself derived from Donna Haraway's *The Cyborg Manifesto*), coupling people and machines—and thereby, dehumanizing their subjects. As drivers meld with their cars, they negotiate the roads as disembodied strangers, moving as a unidirectional collective. It is this paradox, uniting people in their separateness, that lent me the sense of belonging to something larger than myself even as I processed an aching loneliness. Flipping channels on the radio, I realized that anyone around me could be listening to the same sugary pop music, changing lanes and accelerating. I felt remarkably less alone speeding over the poured concrete in a steady cruise control. Driving could also be a communal activity.

And as I was able to lose myself in the habitual activity of driving alongside strangers, so was I losing myself in the infrastructure built for it. Ritual, and ritual places, can stimulate that sense of togetherness, congregating people toward a central purpose. Driving is the American way because it was designed to be, as planners and policy makers prioritized automobiles at every level in the twentieth century, allowing cars to go faster and farther, taking people on solitary journeys through the vast continental expanse of possibility. On the Jersey Turnpike, which I had ridiculed and resented since childhood for its failed promise to be a "Garden State," I found a surprising comfort in its striking architectural loneliness. It was transparent in what it could give: expansive stretches of open road and millions of people just like me, separated by steel frames and an arm's length of distance.

The Turnpike was not built in 1949 to facilitate my grieving process, but navigating the highway decades later with a shared language of turn signals, passing, and cruise control felt like a communicative ritual. Driving home from Philly to Queens on the same road as always, I was not alone at all.

As the plane descended, Carmen thought about how it'd been over a decade since she last saw her brother.

November 1973.

Havana on the Hudson
by Alexandra Beguez

Walking down the winding corridors of JFK, she became anxious at the prospect of seeing everyone after so much time apart. Would being all together feel like it used to, back in Cuba?

CARMITA!

¡PAPI! ¡MIGUELITO!

The last family member she'd seen was her dad over a year ago. They emigrated from Cuba together, staying with his brother in Madrid.

Now the only person left in Cuba was Lazaro, her husband. She prayed it wouldn't be much longer until they reunited.

Weehawken, NJ.

It took a village to help Carmen and her family reach the US.

Welcome home, mi'ja.

I've missed you all so much!

Miguelito and his wife, Mindy, were the first to arrive in the U.S. thanks to The International Rescue Committee (IRC), a nonprofit that provides emergency aid and long-term assistance to refugees. The resettlement program paid for their flight from Madrid to NYC and helped with their green card application.

October 22, 1962.

The IRC also set them up in a hotel for a few days while they searched for an apartment.

Breaking news: President Kennedy has ordered a naval blockade of Cuba to prevent further Soviet missiles from reaching the island nation.

His ten years experience in banking and knowledge of IBM computers quickly landed him a job as an accountant at Chase Manhattan Bank.

After living in Brooklyn for two years, Miguelito and Mindy moved to Weehawken, NJ. They were drawn to the area's fast-growing, tight-knit Cuban community and convenient commute to lower Manhattan.

August 1963.

A small community of about 2,000 Cubans settled in Union City after the 1940s, attracted by the vast job opportunities provided by the over 400 local factories and embroidery mills.

Hudson County had been gradually losing population as urban decline and post-war prosperity led to more people moving out to the suburbs. Many stores on Bergenline Avenue, the main shopping district, were empty.

When it became certain Castro wasn't going anywhere, there was a mass exodus to the US. The US created a resettlement program known as Freedom Flights in cooperation with the Cuban government, transporting refugees to Miami

In 1966, Congress passed the Cuban Adjustment Act (CAA), providing direct financial assistance and allowing Cubans who were already naturalized or had permanent residence to bring their families to the U.S.

Miguelito quickly petitioned to bring thirteen family members to the US. The first to arrive were his mom, Conchita, and sister, Carita, in 1966. They were followed by his older sister, Maria Luisa, and her son, Ulises, over a year later.

Carmen, her husband, and Miguel Sr. decided to stay in Cuba. When their petitions expired, they had to find another way to emigrate to the U.S. Carmen arrived with humanitarian parole on the basis of her sister Carita having Progressive MS.

The arrival of Cuban emigres made an immediate impact.

By 1975, there were more Cubans living in Union City than in any other U.S. city.

After her seasonal work ended, she got a job at a small Cuban-owned embroidery mill on Summit Avenue for a few months, keeping her eyes open for a higher paying union job.

1975.

Soon after, Carmen found permanent employment at Rightman Factory* in Union City. At its height, almost 500 people were employed there with the majority being Cuban and Puerto Rican.

¡Oye! My wife says thank you for the flan.

I'm glad you both liked it!

Like in other textile mills, they wove the fabrics, made the patterns, cut, sewed, and ironed the clothing. The finished products were shipped to luxury department stores in California.

Ireida, the needle keeps jamming.

Try keeping the fabric taut as you feed it in...

There were so many manufacturing jobs available, it was said if you weren't fond of your current employer, you could walk to the nearest factory after lunch and get hired on the spot.

If the new position wasn't to your liking, the next day you could go back to your old job and none would be the wiser.

Carmen earned almost $2 an hour (near the minimum wage) and often worked fifty hour weeks to earn overtime. She considered it a decent wage for someone who spoke little English.

*Factory name cannot be verfied.

When a position opened at Chase Bank, Miguelito encouraged her to apply. She passed on the offer, however, ashamed she wasn't fluent in English like her brother.

You finished your pile and then some. Great job today!

Spending most of her time among fellow Spanish-speakers, as well as her embarrassment over how she sounded, meant there was no sense of urgency to keep practicing.

Sabes, you'd feel more confident speaking English if you enrolled in a class.

I know, I know. But I just signed up for extra hours at work.

I'm saving up for Lazaro's visa. It's very expensive

Maria Luisa ended up applying and got the job.

Maybe I'll sign up next month.

Not that one couldn't get around speaking only Spanish.

Hola Florina, how are you and your parents doing?

Bien! We finally settled into our apartment on Boulevard East.

Camarones enchilados for me.

Tamal en cazuela por favor.

Could I have the ropa vieja?

At one point, over 90% of the businesses on Bergenline Avenue were Cuban-owned.

Florina's mom, much like Carmen, was able to get around and find work despite not knowing English.

How does your mom like it at the bridal shop?

"She made fast friends with her coworkers and says her manager is very kind. Everyone speaks Spanish so she feels welcomed."

I also started working at the Bergen Community Action Program in Teaneck.

That's great!

While the Cuban contribution to the economy and liveliness of North Hudson was valued, not everyone was happy with all the changes that came with it.

One complaint given by the non-Cuban residents was the prevalence of the Spanish language in signage, schools, and local newspapers.

There's a page in Spanish now! They never printed pages in Italian for us.

How are they ever going to learn English?

Complaints about bilingualism aside, without the Cubans and other Latine communities that followed, the area would have continued to lose population and likely never have recovered economically.

RESTAURANT ElArt

Hasta luego, Florina! Tell your mom we said hello!

I will! See you soon!

Like other exile communities, the Cubans who came to Hudson County brought their culture with them and created a new life with the cards they were dealt.

Eventually they, too, took off for the suburbs nearby. They sold their businesses to Colombians, Dominicans, and Ecuadorians, themselves eager to start new lives.

I'm in the mood for a cafe con leche. Want one?

Yes, please.

While they no longer make up the majority of the population, Hudson County is still considered the symbolic heart of the Cuban exile community.

Fin.

Finding Religion in New Jersey

BOB VARETTONI

In my suburban hometown in Bergen County, I count 37 devotional lawn shrines to Mother Mary, 53 octagonal ADT Security door signs, and 108 American flags. There are also 7 churches. I've taken photos of every one.

New Jersey's most redeeming quality is the opportunity it gives everyone to find religion just about everywhere. Even the state's sounds and smells are ecumenical: angry traffic, evening crickets, carnivals, farm machinery and horses, leaf blowers, and lawn mowers. New Jersey's incense ranges from the profane (the Turnpike drive through the Meadowlands) to the sacred (the drive to any shore town when you begin to smell the Atlantic Ocean). Holy water here contains salt. Suffice it to say, I once had a religious experience listening to a folksinger's heartfelt cover of Springsteen's "Thunder Road" at a winery on a Sunday afternoon.

So forgive me if I find religion—or at least solace—in taking photos of local church buildings. This seemingly whimsical obsession amuses my wife. She has become so accustomed to my suddenly pulling the car

Bob Varettoni taking a photograph of St. Joseph's Church, Bogota. Photo by Nancy Varettoni.

over during our "date night" travels that she created an Instagram account where she posts pictures of me taking pictures of churches—like the one of me on a rainy night in Bogota, New Jersey, in front of St. Joseph's Church, which is down the block from Lola's Tattoo Shop on Main Street and not far from where my wife and I had our first apartment, a large one-bedroom. At the time, we didn't have bedroom furniture, so we left it unfurnished and called it a ballroom. Neither of us can dance.

My favorite church is the Cathedral Basilica of the Sacred Heart in Newark, which opened in October 1954 and was the site of my parents' wedding on Thanksgiving Day 1955. People flock to nearby Branch Brook Park every April for the Cherry Blossom Festival. New Jersey has more cherry trees than Washington, DC, with over twenty-seven hundred bursting into full bloom each spring. It doesn't matter to this church. This church is always in full bloom. Its magnificence is such that my mother, upon finding out she could secure the cathedral for her wedding, sought permission from her pastor in Garfield not to have her ceremony at her family's local church on Lanza Avenue. Instead, Mom arranged for her immigrant Polish-speaking parents to take the first limo ride of their lives to travel to Newark, where her bridesmaids needed to stitch together two red carpets to cover the distance down the long center aisle. Mom's wedding was an American fairy tale made possible by my wife's great-grandfather. He was one of the Irish day laborers who laid the stones when the cathedral's construction began at the turn of the century. My Babci was in tears when she beheld Sacred Heart. It appeared to her then, as it does to me now, the closest place to heaven in New Jersey.

Churches are like that. They connect us with past generations, and nowhere more so than when you find a church with an adjoining graveyard. (Churches have "graveyards," while "cemeteries" are burial sites not on church grounds.)

In New Jersey, the dead outnumber us. North Arlington, where the living population is sixteen thousand, is also—thanks to Holy Cross Cemetery—the final resting place for three hundred thousand souls. More than ninety-six thousand people are buried in the town where I grew up,

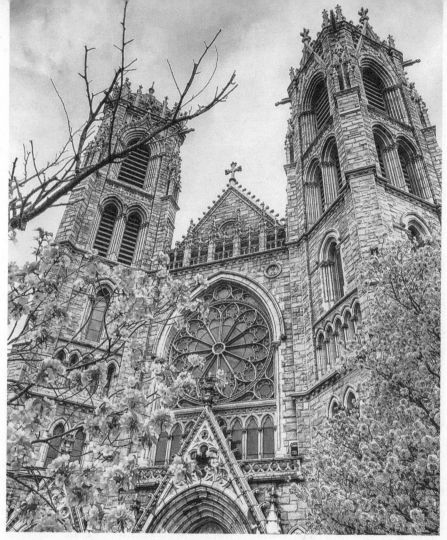

Cathedral Basilica of the Sacred Heart, Newark

Church of the Atonement, Tenafly

Totowa, a borough with a population of only eleven thousand. Once I took Mom to place a palm wreath beside Dad's gravestone there. "I'm getting tired, Bob," she said to the ground, not to me, for both our names are the same: "I want to go home." In mortal life, nothing lasts forever. Meanwhile, churches overlooking graveyards are haunting monuments to our longing for permanence and redemption and our innate belief that love lasts forever.

Like great art, a church's beauty lasts forever. This is the case with the Church of the Atonement at dusk in Tenafly; you can easily find such a church in Montclair or Clinton or Summit or in any of the other picturesque towns across New Jersey.

What especially interests me, however, is the sustaining beauty of form and spirit of inner-city churches in sometimes-now-impoverished communities. Our Lady of Fatima sits on the opposite side of Newark's Cathedral Basilica and railroad tracks, off an unusually busy side street in a largely Portuguese neighborhood called The Ironbound. I was unable to take a photo here without people in it because neighbors kept taking turns to stand in prayer in front of the statue above the main entrance. This is not the generic Mary adorning the lawns of my hometown. It's the specific Mary who appeared to three children in Fatima, Portugal, on the thirteenth of each month from May through October 1917. They saw Mother Mary hover above an oak tree where they had been herding sheep. Decades later, pilgrims to The Ironbound believe that if they pray to Our Lady of Fatima, she will intercede with God on their behalf.

The churches in and around Newark have made compromises over the years, but they have never surrendered. The towers of St. Adalbert's in Elizabeth were dismantled in 1981 due to damage caused by the constant vibration of low-flying aircraft at nearby Newark Airport. For the same reason, St. Patrick's in Elizabeth needed to remove the crosses atop its two majestic front spires.

In Jersey City, I took a photo inside St. Mary of the Immaculate. Its

St. Patrick's, Elizabeth

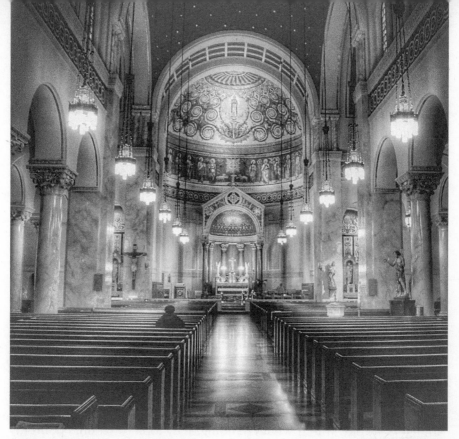

St. Mary of the Immaculate, Jersey City

doors were unlocked the cold Saturday I visited, and some people found comfort there. Unlocked churches, often in inner cities, have warm hearts. At St. Bonaventure's Church in Paterson, where Mom and I listen to the Chopin Singing Society Male Choir of Passaic perform each Epiphany Sunday, the Franciscan friars unlock its doors so that the homeless might have sanctuary. Other city churches have been converted to other uses, or they are behind fences, in disrepair. Their spires, crosses, statues, and towers perpetually loom, usually unnoticed, over all the commerce and street life below. They may not always provide protection, but they never pass judgment.

New Jersey's churches are tangible reminders of transcendence amid everyday life. They stand amid poverty of spirit or means, for some of the most ornate structures I've seen are in the poorest neighborhoods. Their architecture is sometimes sturdy and utilitarian and sometimes breathtaking, but every building invokes our better angels in expressions of hope and longing.

This feels especially poignant as I write this at the end of summer 2020, when so many of us feel hopeless and lost. I confess, there may not be exactly thirty-seven Marys adorning the lawns in New Milford. I tried to count them as I roamed often-empty streets these past few months. But my mind wandered.

Churches tell us, defiantly, that there is more to life than this.

Whenever I pull my car over and run out to take a photo of a church, strangers stop to watch what I'm doing. They look to where I point my camera. I like to think they marvel at what they see and wonder why they hadn't noticed it before.

It's easy to find religion in New Jersey. It requires no particular belief. Just look up, remember the folksinger's heartfelt song, and show a little faith.

Finding Home

JEN A. MILLER

In 2017, I set out to see the fifty states I hadn't been to yet. I did so after my dog died, right about when the worst neighbor dispute my realtor had ever seen forced me to sell my home. Why not pack up and do this thing that my grandparents had also done in 1990 after my uncle died and, along the way, find another place to live that was not New Jersey? I'd been thinking about it for more than a year, as soon as water from holes in my neighbor's roof started to drip into my bedroom ceiling via a wall we shared, as if it was a sign from above that I needed to try something new.

I took this series of unfortunate events—the loss of the house, the loss of the dog, the loss of whatever it was that had given me a feeling of "home" in that house for more than a decade, and in that state for all of my life—and turned them into a grand adventure, a new start.

It was something I could do because I had no house, no dog, no job where I needed to physically be somewhere—and, as I said over and over again when explaining my quest, no family. I was thirty-seven and single with no kids. If you look up the demographics of the American family from the Pew Research Center, the focus is on parents and number of kids in the home, as if those of us who aren't part of that kind of unit have floated away like balloons from a careless child's hand. Except, of course, I had a family: three siblings, six nephews, two dozen cousins, two still-living parents, and two grandparents. But I didn't have my "own" family, I thought.

I left on Memorial Day weekend and drove all over this country. I walked through a prairie in Oklahoma, hiked in the water of the Narrows at Zion National Park, laid out at a topless pool in Las Vegas in 120 degree heat, and then flew to Hawaii the next day. I stayed with a friend whose father brought the women flowers for their hair in the morning, picked from their garden, where they also grew their own lemons and coffee. And in Idaho, I found another perfect-for-me dog.

While I could feel the tug of things I was missing at home in New Jersey—things like strawberry picking on Memorial Day weekend, my dad's men's-league baseball game double header on Father's Day, the first day when it's really not too cold to swim in the ocean—I felt I couldn't go back. I decided to get a temporary rental in Boulder and prepared to stake a new claim in a place where I could train for my next 50K trail run (or beyond, because everyone ran really far in Boulder!) without the worry of a New Jersey summer's usual dreck. Moving to Colorado would be the first step in a fresh life for me, far away from that block in New Jersey where my home had been yanked away. My friend had moved to the Netherlands; surely I could move half a country away. How hard could it be?

But my friend moved to the Netherlands with her husband and daughter. I moved to Boulder with a dog. We squashed into a one-bedroom condo that resembled a hundred other condos in the same complex, in a town spilling over its edges to add more more more, and where I knew not one soul. I was used to densely packed suburbs. One of the things I liked about my old town was that it felt like a community because you were never that far from the next person. But Boulder was too jammed, too packed, and being able to escape into the mountains didn't unclench that tightness when I lay in my rental bed at night and tried to go to sleep; I fell into a misery I haven't felt since my freshman year of college in Florida. Then, though, I'd moved because I had a goal: to get a college degree, and I'm glad I stuck it out. But what was the goal in Boulder? To not feel humidity anymore? I was going to divert my entire life to another part of the country because I wanted be better at a sport that's a hobby? I had planned to be there for two months to see how it felt. It took four days for me to decide that feeling was "no."

I drove back to New Jersey in three days, and as I pulled up in front of my mom's house, I did a thing I hate when other people do it: I blared the horn like mad yelling, "I AM HOME!" She didn't hear because she was watching *America Ninja Warrior*, but luckily I still had a key to open her front door.

I did a little more traveling after that, trying to figure where I could go and start again but still be near the core people in my life. Instead of casting around looking for something I'd already had, the summer after my trip I bought a house in a different New Jersey town not far from the one I sold, near my mom, my dad, my grandmom, my siblings and aunts and uncles and cousins and nephews and the friends I've had since high school. I'm busy with painting and contractors and furniture shopping and rediscovering clothes and books and tchotchkes and plates that have been in boxes for more than a year. I am finally, once again, home.

Illustration by Alex Flannery

My Favorite Devil

ERICA COMMISSO

"I hate Alex Mogilny, Dad."

I remember the words slipping from my mouth, filled with all the rage my six-year-old self could muster. I was sitting in my modest living room in suburban Toronto, and my father and I had just watched Mogilny, who wore number 89 for the New Jersey Devils, score against our native Maple Leafs' then-goaltender, Curtis Joseph. It would probably cost them the game, my juvenile NHL analytics skills surmised. Turns out, I was right, and Mogilny scored an overtime game-winner to lift the Devils over the Leafs that regular-season game.

The Devils were on fire then, winning the Stanley Cup in the 1999–2000 season and dominating the Eastern Conference with big contributions from their lineup, rife with stars like Mogilny, Patrik Elias, Scott Niedermayer, and Martin Brodeur.

I loved hockey from the day I was born, and I was grandfathered into Toronto Maple Leafs fandom by my father and my birthplace. It was fun to watch the games until they lost to the Philadelphia Flyers in the second round of the playoffs, which felt like it happened every year. So I got to thinking. And, I decided, I didn't hate Alex Mogilny after all. I admired the grace with which he moved the puck, his keen scoring eye, how well he could pass it. I appreciated that he made it all look so easy. I decided that Alex Mogilny was now my favorite player.

I enjoyed watching him play, and I took for granted the Stanley Cup I watched him hoist over his head, the awards I watched him win, the records I watched him break. I followed him when, in a piece of weird luck, he signed with the Maple Leafs. Knowing it would make me a Leafs fan again, my family immediately bought me my first Maple Leafs jersey bearing Mogilny's name for my ninth birthday. I went back to the Devils when he re-signed there, deciding that I was more loyal to him, the magician on ice, than I was to any team. I spent time at the Hockey Hall of Fame looking for snippets of information about him. I knew he was considered legendary, of course, but I was too young to understand that even the legendary players don't last forever.

Mogilny's last NHL season was incomplete. He got hurt, and to recover, he was sent to the Devils' AHL affiliate, then the Albany River Rats. He lit up the minor league team but never went back to the NHL. He never officially retired, but he never played again.

Alexander Mogilny was born in the Soviet Union in 1969. He played with Pavel Bure and Sergei Federov for the Soviet Union's national team and was quickly dubbed a superstar. But because of the Soviet rules at the time, it was unlikely that any player under its umbrella would ever play in the NHL. Soviet draft picks were considered throwaways. That was until Alex Mogilny became the first player to defect from the Soviet Union.

He was drafted eight-ninth overall by the Buffalo Sabres in 1988 and, in the middle of an international tournament, willfully kidnapped by members of the Sabres' management team and brought to Buffalo. He made history when he played his first NHL game on October 5, 1989. He quickly made history again, scoring his first goal on his first shift in the first minute of the first period of his first game. He went on to set ten other Sabres records before he was traded to Vancouver because of issues with the Russian mob. Mogilny's old friend Pavel Bure played in Vancouver by that point, and the Canucks were equipped to handle the mob following Russian players around attempting to extort them.

By the time Mogilny found himself in New Jersey, he had broken several records, impressed fans and players around the league, and dealt with more international turmoil than almost anyone else in the league. He was hard to miss on the ice but increasingly evasive with the media. He was great, but he knew there was more to life than hockey. So when he went back to New Jersey for the second time and quietly slipped into unofficial retirement, I wasn't shocked. It was a Mogilny move.

I had new favorite players over the years, men who provided me with adequate entertainment but who paled in the face of Mogilny's talent. The Devils weren't the force they used to be; but they had given me Mogilny, so I was fiercely loyal. Starting in my early twenties, I even flew to New Jersey a few times a season to watch games in the Prudential Center, where I could finally cheer with like-minded fans.

On one of my trips to a Devils game, I spent time in Hoboken. Walking through the brownstone homes and along the waterfront gave me a sense of peace, trust, and belonging that was unfamiliar to me. It felt like home. And so, a few months after my trip, I packed up my things and moved into my first apartment in the Mile Square town, uptown and right by the Hudson River. Fittingly, I attended the Devils' home opener a short while later.

November 2017, a few months after I moved, was a tough blow for my fandom, though. Alex Mogilny won a lawsuit against the New Jersey Devils for failing to follow proper concussion protocol. It turned out that the time he was sent down to the River Rats was because Lou Lamoriello, the general manager at the time, refused to get him tested for a head injury. The lawsuit awarded Mogilny a relatively small chunk of change and tarnished my opinion of the team. A few days later, the Devils traded one of my modern-day favorite players, Adam Henrique, who carried the team to the Stanley Cup final as a rookie in 2012. I sat in shock, wearing my jersey signed by half the team, wondering if I could ever again cheer for a team that had dealt me these two blows in a week. Then I looked out my window onto a beautiful, quiet Hoboken street and remembered how thankful I was to the team that brought me to my true home.

Somewhere in New Jersey

DAN MISDEA

"Hey, don't I know you from somewhere?"

"I'm not here to destroy *this* city – I just stopped
to pick up some pizza."

"The breadcrumbs here are good, but you _have_ to try this little park in Nutley."

"Tonight, live from Metuchen, we'll finally find what we've all been looking for: the truth."

"The Fields! The Orchards! The Roads! The Lanes!"

Woodbine and the Hirsch Agricultural School

HALLEL YADIN

Later in life, when we were scattered in every part of this big country, we always had with us the tender memories of the happy Woodbine days.

> —Katharine Sabsovich, *Adventures in Idealism: A Personal Record of the Life of Professor Sabsovich*

In 1891, a modest group of Russian Jewish refugees—about fifty families comprising three hundred people—arrived in southern New Jersey. They were allotted fifty acres each, on which they could till the loamy soil. This was their allocation for a new life in the United States.

Farmers in Vineland. From the archives of the YIVO Institute for Jewish Research.

The Woodbine colony was founded by the German railroad financier Baron Maurice de Hirsch in response to anti-Jewish riots called "pogroms," which swept Russia in the late nineteenth century and precipitated a wave of Jewish migration to the United States. A related Jewish "back to the land" movement was coalescing at the same time, largely in response to pogroms and violent persecution in Russia and elsewhere. Woodbine colonists were especially influenced by the Russian movement Am Olam, which encouraged Jews to settle in agricultural colonies in the United States. Woodbine was the first, and the Baron de Hirsch Fund would go on to establish similar, immensely influential projects throughout the United States and South America. Woodbine is also considered one of the most successful Jewish settlements of this period, and in 1903, it became the first autonomous Jewish settlement in the United States.

The school established there, the Hirsch Agricultural School (HAS) was the first secondary agricultural school in the United States. Founded in 1894, HAS was tuition-free, though not a public school, and its students had to pass Cape May County's final examinations to graduate. Its alumni scattered all around the country, doing farmwork from Rhode Island to Wisconsin to Montana. Some went on to remarkable achievements, like Jacob Lipman, who was an influential director of the New Jersey Agricultural Experiment Station. Beyond his own contributions to agricultural science, it was there that he took Selman Waksman, who would later win the Nobel Prize for curing tuberculosis, under his wing. (Waksman, mind you, was also a Russian-born Jew.)

Woodbine and HAS were at their core a New Jerseyan project. Logistically, the South Jersey terrain made sense for the colony's needs. Land was cheap, well suited for a variety of crops, and in close proximity to markets in New York City and Philadelphia. The region made sense socially as well. By the time of Woodbine's establishment, New Jersey was well on its way to becoming the state that it is today: one of the most diverse states in the country, with one of the highest proportions of foreign-born immigrants, disproportionately Jewish, and still quite rural land-wise. Furthermore, the first Jewish farm colony in North America, Alliance, had recently been established in South Jersey. Jewish farming played a key role in South Jersey's agriculture overall throughout the first half of the twentieth century. The state's Jewish agricultural scene developed rapidly in this time period. Official and unofficial Jewish farms dominated in certain agricultural areas, especially poultry. Conversely, South Jersey was the key launching pad for Jewish agricultural movements throughout the United States.

New Jersey has also been home to a captivating array of utopian experiments: Helicon Home Colony, the experimental colony that Upton Sinclair created with his proceeds from *The Jungle*, which only lasted for a year until it burned down; Stelton, Piscataway's anarchist commune; Monroe's Physical Culture City, a utopian fitness community; the list goes on.

New Jersey's education system (along with everything else in the state) has historically been highly localized. HAS is but one of many experimental schools established throughout the state's history.

Life at HAS

Woodbine colonists had escaped violent antisemitism, and as much as they wanted their children to be safe, they also wanted to see them

The *H.A.S. Record*, February 1918 edition, page 40. From the Library of the YIVO Institute for Jewish Research.

thrive in the United States. Alumni were encouraged—one might even say *noodged*—to write in and share their successes with the *H.A.S. Record*, the school's yearbook.

HAS was also a site to forge an American Jewish identity. In some ways, this came naturally, almost inevitably, to the students. They went on trips to Sea Isle and New York City alongside the Maccabean Festival and Zion Circle Meetings. They put on English-language plays while fundraising for the Woodbine Jewish Relief Fund. They partook in local high school sports leagues and Halloween parties, speaking circles and local poultry shows through the Washington Feather Club. (The Feather Club is not to be confused with Club Feathers, River Edge's gay nightclub, which would not be established until 1978.)

However, these elements of "typical" American life were not nearly as compelling as the image of the Jew as a farmer. Students were implored to trumpet their agrarian success; in fact, this was one of the explicit purposes of the *Record*. The February 1915 issue states, "It is through the RECORD we want to spread the progress of this school and the Jewish agriculturalist in general.... The further aim of the RECORD is to impress upon the public, that the Jew 'means business,' when he goes into agriculture, and that he is here to stay."

The agricultural identity afforded by South Jersey was also, frankly, a fundamental part of persecuted Jews remediating their *own* self-image. In the February 1915 issue, Professor J. A. Rosen wrote, "The foundation strata of a healthy and vigorous nation are the agricultural elements.... If we [Jews] are ever to regain our might as vigor as a nation, we must press our heart to Mother Earth. In this national movement, the Hirsch Agricultural School can, and must play an important part." The role of place in this process is unmistakable. Indeed, in a 1917 valedictory address, Maxwell B. Cohen wrote of "the surroundings": "which have become a part of us! The fields! The orchards! The roads! The lanes!"

Woodbine's Legacy

Woodbine, like virtually every Jewish farm settlement in the United States established during this era, did not survive in its intended form. By 1919, most of the "manufactories" that supplemented agricultural income had closed. By 1929, the Hirsch Fund had pulled out entirely. The colonists held on, but Woodbine became a more typical small town; and many of the original Jewish families left in the post–World War II suburb boom.

Woodbine's legacy endures in tangible and intangible ways. The Woodbine Brotherhood Synagogue now houses Stockton University's Sam Azeez Museum of Woodbine History. The streets are still laid out in the grid first conceptualized in 1891. Jewish back-to-the-land movements are still present today, albeit in different forms.

As for HAS, the school closed in 1917 amid the upheaval of World War I. It became the Woodbine Developmental Center, which provides services to men with developmental disabilities and is now the largest employer in Cape May County.

In 1901, William Stainsby, chief of New Jersey's Bureau of Statistics, wrote that the Woodbine colonists had been considering putting up a monument to the Baron. "The question of erecting an elegant marble monument to Baron de Hirsch has been agitated at the colony," he noted, "but what need of that?"

"This," he wrote, "is his monument."

Seasons Eatings

KAE LANI PALMISANO

Food is a story of time and place. A bite of seafood can transport you to a coastal fishing town, a fresh salad of greens and tart berries can signal spring giving way to summer, and a hearty soup of wild game and root vegetables can give you a sense of a rustic and rural winter. Though these dishes are distinct, each perfectly expresses New Jersey's changing landscapes and revolving seasons and illustrates the nuanced characteristics that lend generously to its official nickname of the Garden State.

"New Jersey is a beautiful garden," says Melissa Hamilton.

"It's so rich with food," adds Christopher Hirsheimer. "We're surrounded by beautiful farms and gorgeous produce."

Hamilton and Hirsheimer are the creative forces behind Canal House, a New Jersey–based cookbook-publishing company and photography studio that expanded to add a restaurant in 2019, the Canal House Station. Working in an old railroad station on the banks of the Delaware River in Milford, New Jersey, the James Beard Award–winning cooks draw inspiration from the state's bountiful seasons.

"What the area offers us is what we're cooking," explains Hamilton.

"The thing with cooking with the seasons is that you get to see your old favorites come back again. Just as the tomatoes start to go out of season, you're kind of tired of them anyway, and you're ready to move on to the root vegetables, the squashes, and the apples."

I couldn't agree more with their sentiment. Having grown up in New Jersey, I've noticed that my own cravings are in tune with the seasons. As a kid, part of my normal routine was picking fresh zucchini, cucumbers, eggplants, peppers, and tomatoes from the garden in my backyard. I instinctively knew that strawberries in June led to blueberries in July, and when the grapes were about to burst off the vine during the hottest days of August, it was just about time to start canning for the fall and winter. This kind of culinary circadian rhythm didn't dawn on me until I moved back to New Jersey after nearly a decade of living in Philadelphia. Though I had moved to Philadelphia to get closer to its food scene, the city life had created distance between me and the joy of eating with the seasons.

Cities tend to be cultural hubs where food trends percolate, and though Philadelphia has recently earned national attention, New York City has always been recognized as an epicenter for food culture. New York City's food scene is an engine fueled by world-class chefs and the food media entities that cover them. When one shoots up, the other follows like a piston alternating to move the city and its culinary influence forward. Hamilton and Hirsheimer were part of that engine when they met as food-magazine editors in New York City, but their work always stood out from the rest. In a culinary landscape focused on the allure of the seemingly unattainable, Hamilton and Hirsheimer, who were at *Saveur* magazine at the time, were grabbing people's attention with approachable and attainable dishes that connected readers to the common threads of the human experience. "It's the same story over and over again," says Hirsheimer, *Saveur*'s cofounder and editor. "Every recipe worth its salt has a great story behind it. It's a human story of people," she says.

The fact they've chosen to set up shop in Milford, New Jersey, subverts expectations. Though Milford is only seventy miles west of New York City, the rolling hills and rural farmlands that lead to it make this small town feel worlds away. But it's a charming town with a little main street lined with independently owned shops. It's a familiar setting where Hamilton and Hirsheimer can serve up familiar stories of seasonal favorites—stories in which people could see themselves, because, despite what New York City media says, not everyone lives in the big city. "We want people to identify and to see something they'll recognize that makes them feel like they can do it too," says Hirsheimer. "And they can!"

It's a sense of nostalgic familiarity that appears in their writing, their cooking, and even their photography. Over the years, they have become known for their uniquely carefree, somewhat unpolished yet effortlessly elegant, aesthetic in how they prepare and present food. Hirsheimer, the photographer of the duo, composes photographs that bring out the beautiful imperfections of home-cooked meals, all plated next to windows flooded by natural light.

Their cookbooks, *Canal House Cooks Every Day* and *Canal House: Cook Something: Recipes to Rely On*, to name just two, are filled with moments that feel like they're plucked out of everyday cooking—juices of a braised beef brisket run into the wells of a generously used wooden cutting board, a bit of yolk is left on a fork and knife next to a freshly cut poached egg on top of a corned beef hash, and the lip of an enamel pot is lightly crusted with red sauce. They're scenes of a homely kitchen that could be yours, featuring real-life dishes that you could make. "We both prefer to have things not perfect because it feels real," says Hamilton.

After years of bringing other people's food stories to life through their work in New York City, they made a decision: "It was time to find a studio out here and see if we could bring the work to us, instead of us traveling far to get to the work, and to begin to tap into our own repertoire," says Hamilton. That sense of no-fuss realness was what drew them to New Jersey. "New Jersey is incredibly beautiful, very unspoiled, very natural, and unaffected," says Hirsheimer, "and of course, that's what we love. It's real!"

There were two other chapters of Canal House, one in Lambertville and one in Frenchtown, before the duo settled in their Milford location. Reinvigorating an old building, being next to the Delaware River, tending to a small garden, and setting up shop in a small, working town in New Jersey have always been important parts of their story, but the new, unexpected twist has been their restaurant, Canal House Station. "It was a natural extension," explains Hamilton. "We did not always want a restaurant, but we wanted a studio space and wanted to be able to interact with the public more frequently. And when we found this old railroad station, it kept saying, 'This has to be a restaurant,' so we added that to the mix."

Their cookbooks have always been about cooking with the seasons, and their restaurant does the same, bringing delectable dishes off the page and onto the plate. Canal House Station is an intimate project that draws connections between the seasonal bounties of New Jersey and the small riverside communities they serve.

The relationship between food and culture is symbiotic. For as much as food is an expression of culture, it is also a force that, like any art form, can dictate culture. And though food is a story about time and place, it can only be expressed and experienced through people. What we eat and how we eat it become a reflection of who we are, where we come from, and when we were here.

THE **EggOmat**

BY LISA ROSALIE EISENBERG

THE EGG-O-MAT STOOD IN FRONT OF THE WARRENVILLE POULTRY FARM AT 41 MOUNTAIN BOULEVARD.

THANK YOU! ENJOY!

CAMILLO EPSTEIN BUILT IT A FEW YEARS AFTER HE AND HIS WIFE ALICE BOUGHT THE PLACE IN 1946.

FARM FRESH EGGS

BACK THEN, THERE WAS NOWHERE IN TOWN TO GO FOR GROCERIES AT NIGHT OR ON WEEKENDS. THE EGG-O-MAT WAS A WAY TO BUY FRESH EGGS WHEN THE EPSTEINS' REGULAR FARM STAND WAS CLOSED.

FARM

EggOmat

EGGS OF DISTINCTION
24 HOUR SERVICE

IT WORKED LIKE ANY VENDING MACHINE. CUSTOMERS PUT IN COINS, AND GOT EGGS IN RETURN:

FROM HEN TO YOU DAILY
WHITE EGGS
TRY THEM FOR QUALITY

5¢ FOR A DOZEN SMALL EGGS
10¢ FOR MEDIUM
25¢ FOR LARGE
35¢ FOR JUMBO

EggOmat
EGGS OF DISTINCTION
24 HOUR SERVICE

FROM HEN TO YOU DAILY WHITE EGGS
TRY THEM FOR QUALITY

BORED TEENAGERS TRIED TAMPERING WITH THE EGG-O-MAT A FEW TIMES.

SO CAMILLO INSTALLED AN INTERCOM.

BZZT!

IF THE EGG-O-MAT HAD ANY UNWELCOME VISITORS, THE EPSTEINS WOULD HEAR IT FROM THE FARMHOUSE.

CAMILLO AND ALICE HAD LEFT NEW JERSEY FOR FLORIDA BY THE TIME MY FAMILY MOVED TO WARREN IN 1994.

IT KIND OF LOOKS LIKE A CALVIN AND HOBBES STRIP OUT HERE.

DOES THAT MEAN YOU'RE STARTING TO LIKE IT?

NO. IT'S BORING AND FULL OF YUPPIES. I DON'T GET WHY WE COULDN'T STAY IN MAPLEWOOD.

SIGH.

LISA, WE'VE BEEN OVER THIS.

I SAW THE REMAINS OF THE EGG-O-MAT AS ONE OF THE FEW COOL PARTS OF MY OTHERWISE BLAND NEW TOWN.

I THOUGHT MAPLEWOOD WAS A TOWN WITH REAL HISTORY, AND I MISSED IT. I LOVED THE DOWNTOWN, THE SIDEWALKS, THE HOUSES.

IT WAS ALSO A PART OF MY FAMILY HISTORY. MY DAD AND HIS PARENTS MOVED THERE FROM NEIGHBORING NEWARK IN 1962.

HIS PARENTS WERE BORN AND RAISED IN WEEQUAHIC, NEWARK'S JEWISH NEIGHBORHOOD, AND STAYED UNTIL MY DAD WAS JUST ABOUT TO START HIGH SCHOOL.

SAUL-GRANDPA

SCOTT-DAD

MIRIAM-GRANDMA

MARC-UNCLE

BUT THEY WOULD ALSO VISIT MY FUTURE HOME OF CENTRAL JERSEY, BUYING EGGS FROM THE COMMUNITY OF JEWISH POULTRY FARMERS THERE.

COHEN'S FARM

2/50¢

EGGS

FARMERS LIKE THE EPSTEINS.

FARM

SCOTTY, HOLD THESE WHILE I GO GET MY PURSE.

CAMILLO AND ALICE FLED VIENNA IN 1938, AFTER THE NAZIS ANNEXED AUSTRIA.

BY 1940, THEY WERE LIVING IN WEEQUAHIC.

MY FAMILY HAD ALSO ESCAPED ANTI-SEMITISM IN EUROPE, YEARS BEFORE THE EPSTEINS' ARRIVAL. NOW THEY WERE NEIGHBORS.

AND CAMILLO AND ALICE WERE JUST A FEW YEARS OLDER THAN MY GRANDPARENTS. DID THEY EVER CROSS PATHS?

MY FAMILY AND THE EPSTEINS HAD WOUND UP IN THE SAME TOWN ONCE AGAIN. I WAS UPSET ABOUT MOVING TO WARREN — BUT FOR THEM, IT WAS A REFUGE.

WARREN HAS CHANGED SINCE THE EGG-O-MAT'S HEYDAY, WITH FARMLAND GIVING WAY TO SUBURBAN SPRAWL.

I WONDER WHAT CAMILLO AND ALICE WOULD THINK OF IT.

THEY MOVED AWAY IN 1980. IN 1989, RENTERS AT THE OLD WARRENVILLE POULTRY FARM PROPERTY WORKED TO MAINTAIN THE EGG-O-MAT'S APPEARANCE — THOUGH IT HAD LONG SINCE STOPPED DISPENSING EGGS.

DESPITE THE EGG-O-MAT'S REGIONAL FAME, IT CONTINUED TO DETERIORATE.

THESE DAYS, IF YOU DRIVE THROUGH DOWNTOWN WARREN, THERE'S NO SIGN OF THE FARM — OR THE EGG-O-MAT.

BUT IT'S STILL AROUND, SITTING IN THE WARREN TOWNSHIP PUBLIC WORKS YARD.

I KNOW THE EGG-O-MAT'S DAYS ARE NUMBERED. BUT THE FACT THAT IT ISN'T TOTALLY GONE BRINGS ME HOPE.

IT'S A VERY NEW JERSEY THING TO ME. FINDING SOMETHING FASCINATING IN A SEEMINGLY MUNDANE LANDSCAPE. A SPECIAL STRANGENESS.

THE EGG-O-MAT REMINDS ME THAT THERE ARE STORIES EVERYWHERE —— SOMETIMES YOU JUST HAVE TO LOOK A LITTLE HARDER FOR THEM.

Illustrations by Kristen Broderick

Fourteen Things You Didn't Know Were Invented in New Jersey

LINDA J. BARTH

1. Reverend Hannibal Goodwin, a Newark minister, had been using glass slides to show Bible scenes to his Sunday-school students, but the glass slides kept breaking. In 1887, working with celluloid in the attic of Plume House, the rectory of the House of Prayer Episcopal Church, Reverend Goodwin invented flexible film, which could be produced and stored in rolls.
2. With Reverend Goodwin's invention of flexible film, Thomas Edison's company created the kinetograph, a motion-picture camera, and the kinetoscope for viewing the movie.
3. In 1953, the Federal Communications Commission approved RCA's color television format. The first television show broadcast in color

was an episode of *Dragnet*, followed by the Tournament of Roses Parade.

4. Thanks to Italo Marchiony's ice cream cone, the container for this yummy treat was now edible! No more glass dishes to wash.

5. Forrest Mars and Bruce Murrie created M&Ms, a chocolate delight perfect for a hot summer day, since they melt in your mouth, not in your hand!

6. To save on the cost of shipping soup, John Dorrance came up with a formula for condensed soup. He removed the water and let cooks add it at home.

7. Thanks to Marc Chavannes and Al Fielding, we can use Bubble Wrap to ship Grandma's fragile teapot to Cousin Emily in one piece. Their little business became Sealed Air, a billion-dollar New Jersey company.

8. Sand was everywhere in Atlantic City, until Alexander Boardman and Jacob Keim came up with a walkway made of boards—the boardwalk!

9. When David Kenney was awarded the patent for a small, portable vacuum cleaner, he credited the prayers he received from the Sisters of Mercy. In thanks, he donated land in the Watchung Mountains for their Mount Saint Mary Academy.

10. Thanks to Willis Carrier for his "Apparatus for Treating Air," or air conditioning, much appreciated on humid summer days in New Jersey.

11. Nursery schoolteacher Kay Zufall realized that a wallpaper cleaner made from a soft, pliable dough was fun for children to use to mold shapes. She called it Play-Doh.

12. Invented way back in 1955 by Bell Labs, solar panels are now seen all over, creating electricity from sunlight.

13. Alexander Cartwright brought his baseball team to New Jersey with new rules: three strikes and you're out, three outs in an inning, fair and foul territory, and equal distance between the bases.
14. The rotary telephone dial, in use for decades, was replaced in 1964 by touch-tone dialing, invented by the scientists at Bell Labs.

Illustration by Tori Wehringer

The Sopranos Family Tour

DONNIE MARTINO

My family had an agreement: once a month, I went to the cemetery where most of my family is buried. I helped tidy up the graves, said my prayers, and listened to whatever scraps of memories my parents were willing to spare on each relative. I was compensated with Italian ice from a nearby bakery. I would slurp fluorescent-pink juice from the bottom of a paper cup as we made our way back home.

One day, when I was ten years old, my father deviated from this routine. He drove past the bakery where we typically stopped, his usual standoffish demeanor giving way to a playful tone as he nearly jumped in his seat.

We drove through the crowded streets of North Arlington, each block crowded with brick buildings and people who weren't spending their weekend reflecting on their dead relatives. Eventually my father pulled over and gestured toward a freestanding brick building with a green sign that read "PIZZALAND" on top of it.

My mother gasped excitedly, asking my father, "Is this it?!"

My father nodded enthusiastically, the two of them turning toward the building and staring at it in awe.

They eventually stopped gawking at this building to explain that this was apparently the same establishment that was featured in the opening credit sequence of *The Sopranos*. I groaned, realizing that I should have known. The show had only been out for a few months, and my parents were obsessed. They were so determined to stay on top of the series that they forced me to go to bed early on Sundays so they could enjoy the gore and sexual content without a preteen potentially walking in on it.

"So are we going to go inside?" I asked, hoping I could get a meal out of this.

"Oh, no! We just wanted to look!" my dad exclaimed. The boyish charm my father displayed moments before dissipated, his posture stiff and his face flat as he started the car again.

At the height of the show's popularity, I decided not to watch *The Sopranos*. As a new-school Italian American kid, I fretted that it glorified the very real struggle we've had with organized crime in our community. As I grew up, I learned painful stories about my family—namely, that I had relatives killed off by the mob—and I decided it was better to honor them by refusing to engage with the media. When the series ended and people were divided by its ending, I laughed, relieved that the reign of *The Sopranos* was finally over.

I never thought I would go back on this claim.

I also didn't really account for being disowned.

The second my conservative Roman Catholic family saw on Facebook that my then-partner had recently transitioned, they learned I wasn't straight. My relationship with my parents immediately became turbulent, complete with terrifying phone calls and ending with me being disowned.

I no longer have access to photographs, recipes, or the elders who taught me so much about my heritage. The only mementos I have from my past are photos from my college graduation, passed along to me the last time I saw my mom. We met at an ice cream parlor, and she explained to me that my father didn't want the images hanging in his shiny new shore house. I contemplated driving up to North Jersey and walking around the landmarks of my childhood, sadly accepting that it could potentially put me in danger. It felt wrong to let go of this part of me, but I couldn't see a way to hang onto it.

One of the first summers after I was disowned, I found myself in need of a show to marathon as I worked on a cosplay project. As I combed through potential streaming options, my hands froze when I saw that *The Sopranos* was available. I couldn't deny that a part of me was curious to finally watch this series. I clicked on the first episode and reminded myself that if it pissed me off, I could always watch something else.

I was unprepared for the overflowing amount of memories that came to my mind as the series began. The opening number featured familiar stretches of the New Jersey Turnpike and, yes, that damn pizzeria my dad dragged me to all those years ago. The exterior shots featuring tight sidewalks and faded painted signs were welcome sights that I assumed I would never be able to see again, out of fear of crossing paths with members of my family. The characters became their own landmarks. When Tony

Soprano donned a cream-colored, ribbed mock turtleneck, it reminded me of every older Italian American man I'd ever known. The many micro-expressions and expertly coiffed hair of Adriana La Cerva made me long for Saturday mornings with my grandma as a similarly presenting woman rubbed black dye into her grayed roots.

Locations became a game for me. I combed through old websites that appeared untouched since they were created a decade ago, trying to decipher whether or not I had visited these locations as a child. Was the bakery featured in season 1, episode 8, the same one that I used to get Italian ice from? Did my parents ever take me to Applegate Farms (featured in season 6, episode 16), or was it another family-owned ice cream shop? Did my dad ever drag me to Fountains of Wayne (featured in season 3, episode 5), or had we gone to a different cement-figure shop? Without access to my family to confirm, I found myself distraught, scrutinizing screenshots and checking Google Maps before I forced myself to close my laptop and sit with what was happening in the show.

I realized that if I stopped trying to force my memories to fit into the setting, I could appreciate them as visuals to replace the photographs I might never see again. My childhood self was correct: the show is violent and spotlights organized crime. Morally corrupt men brandish guns at equally morally corrupt men as they fight over comically large stacks of money. But it's also an exploration of Italian American culture in North Jersey. There are also stretches of highways that remind me of watching raindrops race along the window of my dad's Blazer and indoor swimming pools that looked like the one my high school best friend would invite me to swim in until the bats came out and began to dive toward our heads.

The source material, much like my childhood, is imperfect, but it's what I have to work with.

I'm not sure if I can say *The Sopranos* is one of my favorite shows. Favorite TV shows seem like a genre of small talk that doesn't usually yield itself to massive asterisks that I would have to attach anytime I talk about my relationship with the series. For now, I let it be a memory of sorts I hold close. If I feel comfortable enough sharing more, I will, as if it's a recipe for Christmas cookies or gravy. After all, every family is entitled to a few secrets.

La miramira

HASSAN GHANNY

Running down Main Street in Paterson every ten minutes, you will find a calling card of diaspora: a white jitney bus emblazoned with blue or red signage blasting merengue music. While they stop at NJ Transit bus stops, they are privately run by multiple companies with names like "Spanish Bus" and "Taíno Express." They seat around twenty people, the majority of whom speak English as a second language. The buses travel on public city streets but represent a world privy to almost no one outside Passaic County.

This isn't Jim Jarmusch's *Paterson*. This is the story of the miramira—the lifeline and backbone of communities of color in Passaic County.

I know the route like the back of my hand, all potholes accounted for like blemishes on the skin. The buses leave from gate 56 of the Port Authority Bus Terminal in New York City; you can catch them from across the street, but it's a dollar cheaper to board at the gate. Every time I want to visit home, it seems like the price goes up. I get used to asking to driver, "¿Cuanto pa' Pasey?" Then I take my seat in one row near the rear-middle of the jitney, in the row where the wheel creates a bump on which to rest my feet.

The bus descends into the Lincoln Tunnel and quickly makes landfall in Union City, where it exits Route 495 and makes a jaunt on city streets. The buses from gate 51 turn here, bound for Jersey City down Bergenline Avenue. The jitney driver moves stealthily, picking up passengers while leaping ahead of the NJ Transit buses on the same corridor.

The drivers are unanimously Dominican. One time, an Afro-Caribbean guy, a real Rasta man with a net cap covering his locs, was driving the bus and playing the latest Vybz Kartel. I told this later to my Guyanese friend, and she remarked, "He made Black history with that one!"

Past "Yunionsiri," the bus takes the highway through the Turnpike interchange, passes through the Meadowlands and by the monstrosity that is the Xanadu (you might know it as the American Dream), and in no time turns onto Route 21 in Clifton. Celia Cruz sings "Ríe y Llora" from the stereo as the bus soars over the off-ramp into Passaic Park.

Main Avenue in Passaic Park is an Orthodox Jewish neighborhood. I haven't seen a lot of folks get on or off here, except for one man, one time, who sat across from me and got off at the corner of Main and Van Houten. I remembered him because he pointed out to me that my debit card had fallen out of my wallet, for which I'm still grateful.

Not a moment passes before Main Avenue spills onto uptown Passaic. Clothing stores and eateries line every storefront between State Street and Monroe Street. This stretch of road was once home to a train line; with the train tracks gone, now there are just rows of parking in the middle of the street. Passaic was once a factory town, home of textile mills dotting the Passaic River and clothing stores hocking freshly spun wares. Nearly everyone you meet here is Spanish-speaking, Mexican or Dominican or

Puerto Rican, with cadences in their Spanish speech to match. You quickly learn the dialectal differences; a *pastelito* is an empanada to some people and a cake to others; a *pan dulce* is a given for Mexicans but barely registers to a Colombian, who might ask if you mean *pan de bono*. (They're both delicious.)

This is no suburb or commuter town. Passaic is a mighty place whose day has passed. The mightiest symbol is the long-vacant bank tower at 663 Main Avenue, which towers above the rest of the one- and two-story businesses along the strip. It was empty for as long as I lived in Passaic; the internet tells me there's a fitness gym and a sushi bar on the first floor of the building now. How the mighty have fallen.

My stop is a few streets north of the main strip, at Summer Street. From there, I would walk down to Botany Village and my family's home on President Street, across from the factories. But this bus is headed ever northward, to downtown Paterson. Now the bus is crossing into Clifton, a suburban city with few stories to tell that wouldn't end up in *Weird NJ*. The bus passes discount dollar stores and barbershops before encountering a few curiosities, a baklava bakery and a Peruvian *jato*, that tell you that Paterson is looming ever nearer.

We pass Corrado's, a place where fresh tortillas and ghee and *pastelillos de guayaba* and *huancaína* seasonings all share shelf space. Get your fill now; the rest of the area is a bit of a food desert. (Unless you count C-Town.)

Soon Clifton becomes South Paterson or, as a local might say, "Souf Pete." Here is where every ethnic group blooms. The neighborhood is chiefly Turkish and Palestinian, known to outsiders as "Little Istanbul." I know it as a place to get impeccable Turkish coffee or *adana kebab* from the places I ate as a child. Most of my classmates were Turkish, children of adults who immigrated as political dissidents. I count off Ömer's dad's furniture shop, Aslihan's family's bodega, the apartment building where one of my teachers used to live. Just over the I-80 viaduct from Madison Avenue, the whole place becomes *sazonado* with the flavors of the Spanish Caribbean. But here, everything is halal and tastes of *za'atar*.

We pass Saint Joseph's Hospital and, on the opposite side, the road leading out to Garrett Mountain Reservation. Everyone in the hood has gone on walks and hikes here to see the cliffs that overlook the floodplain on which Paterson is built. One week my senior year of high school, a gargantuan amount of snow melted, and the Passaic River flooded every bridge in Paterson, canceling school. It was temperate that week, and I got off the bus here to go for a walk in Garrett Mountain. The long uphill walk was well worth the break from urban sprawl and some fresh air—as fresh as southern Passaic County gets, anyhow.

The bus passes under a tangle of highways and off-ramps to make landfall in another ethnic enclave, the edge of a Peruvian neighborhood so concentrated that the Peruvian consulate is located here. (Worry not, the Dominican consulate is down the street.) Turn right and you'll get to the (very much underused) NJ Transit station. Look left and you'll see the Passaic County Jail. This isn't a picturesque part of town, but it's familiar—a place I could walk around at 2 a.m. and feel not a twinge of danger. Somewhere on the edge of here is the Great Falls, Paterson's most positive claim to fame. It doesn't bore me per se, but it's not the Paterson I look for when I go.

When the bus hits traffic, you know the ride is almost over. The stretch of Main Street between Market Street and Broadway is practically another country, a concrete Jacmel. Storefronts blast merengue and dembow. Street vendors sell *pastelitos* and cut mango. If you don't hear Spanish spoken, it might be a language from another continent entirely. We pass by both shoddy clothing stores and a three-story thrift store where Claudia and Evan and I would meet to find treasures. When the ride ends on Broadway, you can walk or you can grab the next bus going east—another white jitney that the kids take to go down to Garden State Plaza for work or Friday leisure.

I walk down from Broadway to La Pupusa Loca and think, "This is home—this is what I came for—*gracias por la vida*." Though I left New Jersey at eighteen, the miramira is my passageway to the place I know best and can't ever harken to forget. If you ever want an experience all your own, give the bus a try—just don't forget, in the absence of buttons or pull strings, you will have to yell, "En la próxima parada!" if you want to get off. (If you ever do.)

New Jersey Trivia

So You Think You Know Jersey?

LORRAINE GOODMAN

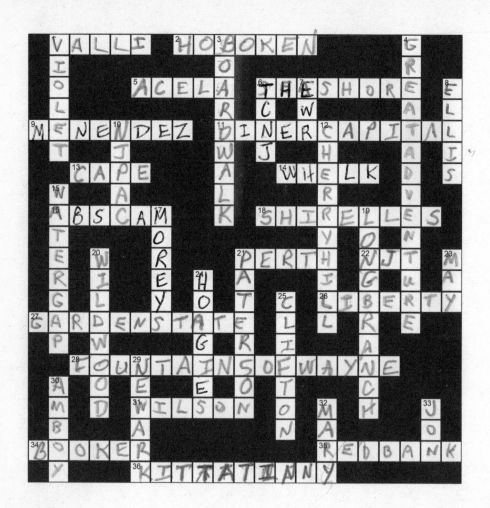

For the puzzle's solution, see the last page of this book.

Across

1 Jersey boy Frankie
2 Jersey city purchased for a half a barrel of beer, twelve kettles, six guns, and more
5 Amtrak train to DC
6 Jersey summer destination
9 Partner of 34 Across (Senator Bobby)
11 Dubious distinction, "_____ of the World"
13 Jersey May
14 New Jersey State Shell, the knobbed ____;
16 Jersey FBI sting of the late '70s
18 '50s–'60s girl group from Passaic
21 Jersey's Amboy
22 Local transport, abbr.
26 Jersey park, overlooking New York Harbor
27 Jersey's nickname
28 American rock band named after a lawn-ornament store in Wayne
31 Woodrow, president of Princeton University
34 Partner of 9 Across (Senator Cory)
35 Borough on the Navesink River
36 Mountain site whose name in the Lenni-Lenape language means "endless mountains" or "Great Mountain"

Down

1 Jersey state flower
3 Historical landmark in Atlantic City
4 Theme park and safari destination
6 State college, abbr.
7 Jersey alternative to LGA
8 ___ Island National Monument
10 Cultural Center, abbr.
12 Home to the headquarters of Subaru of America
15 Delaware ___, separating New Jersey from Pennsylvania
17 ___Piers & Beachfront Waterparks
19 Another beach town, accessible by 22 Across
20 Resort city on the New Jersey coast, home to the National Marbles Hall of Fame
21 Largest city in and the county seat of Passaic County
23 Jersey Cape
24 Heroes and such
25 Neighbor to 21 Down
29 Birthplace of Shaquille O'Neal, Aaron Burr, and Queen Latifah
30 Perth ___, NJ
32 See 34 Across, first name
33 Rock's Bon Jovi

Acknowledgments

For a book with this many contributors and that came into existence over many years, compiling a list of people to thank has been incredibly daunting. Dozens and dozens of people helped turn this idea I had into the actual thing you are holding in your hands, and I am endlessly grateful to each and every one of them.

First of all, thank you to the brilliant contributors to this collection for your time, talent, and stories. Thank you for trusting me and allowing this book to be a home for your voice. Thank you to everyone who was interviewed, provided a photograph, or served as a resource.

All of my gratitude and appreciation to Peter Mickulas, Courtney Brach, Brice Hammack, Andrew Katz, Laura Lassen, Veronica Meliksetian, Vincent Nordhaus, Savannah Porcelli, Blake Ritchie, and the entire team at Rutgers University Press for making this book possible. Thank you to Regina Starace for designing the book's cover and interior, Alex Flannery for the cover's bird illustration, and Maria Alba for my author photo.

Many thanks to current and previous Jersey Collective team members, as well as anyone who has ever participated in the project, attended one of our events, partnered with us in some way, or who follows us on Instagram. Thank you as well to the founders and team members of other Instagram accounts that are a part of the New Jersey Instagram community.

I am grateful for all of the writing teachers I've been lucky enough to learn from over the years, especially Mrs. L (Elizabeth Robin), Allison Tevald, and Kathy Volk Miller. Many thanks to Sari Botton, Samantha Bremekamp, Jeff Campbell, Lilly Dancyger, Peter Genovese, Brian Gresko, Deborah Smith, Rebecca Soffer, and Jason Wilson for their generous anthology or publishing-related advice.

Thank you to my writing classmates over the years for making my work better and showing me new possibilities through theirs.

Thank you to all of my library colleagues past and present.

I would need a lot more pages to list all of the friends I feel lucky to know, a truly good problem to have. I want to acknowledge in particular Sarah Boyd, Kate Brindisi, Rachel Casey, Marissa Chimento, Kamelia (Ani) DeSoucey, Danielle Emrick, Sean Flannery, Stacey Slowinski, Jeff Solomon, Aislinn Tomchak, and Tina Walsh for helping me in both tangible and intangible ways with this book or with previous creative endeavors that paved the way for this one.

I don't think I could ever adequately thank my family, but all of my love and admiration to Carol, Eileen, Daniela, Dave, Gloria, Jim, Mark, Mary Anne, Neil; my cousins Amber, Chelsea, Colin, Dan, Evan, Julia, Kasey, Kate, Liam, Lucy, Pat, Sam, and their partners. And to my parents, whom I *definitely* could never properly thank for their unconditional love and support of everything I've ever wanted to do.

Lastly, to Alex: This is a better book because I was able, during every step of the process, to work through things by talking them out with you. I'm pretty sure I knew I was going to love you when you asked me on a date to tour the state house and get tomato pies. Thank you. For all of it.

Further Reading

New Jersey Fan Club is not the first book about New Jersey, and it won't be the last.

Here is a nonexhaustive list of just a few nonfiction books about our state that I've enjoyed and recommend. They span a variety of topics, from true crime to Action Park to the Jersey Devil to a hiking guide.

I hope you will continue reading about New Jersey, and I hope you will find a way to add your story to the conversation. If you don't feel like you've seen your experience anywhere, then I hope you'll write it (or draw it or photograph it).

Bilby, Joseph G., James M. Madden, and Harry Ziegler. *On This Day in New Jersey History*. Charleston, SC: History Press, 2015.

Buck, Elaine, and Beverly Mills. *If These Stones Could Talk: African American Presence in the Hopewell Valley, Sourland Mountain, and Surrounding Regions of New Jersey*. Lambertville, NJ: Wild River Books, 2018.

Burnett, Robert B., ed. *Pictorial Guide to Victorian New Jersey: 292 Contemporary Engravings from "Harper's," "Frank Leslie's," and*

Other Sources, 1850–1895. Newark: New Jersey Historical Society, 1986.

Delaney, John. *Nova Caesarea: A Cartographic Record of the Garden State, 1666–1888, Including the First Maps, Wall Maps & County Atlases, as Well as Past & Current Views. Commemorating the 350th Anniversary of the Naming of New Jersey*. Princeton, NJ: Princeton University Library, 2014.

Estes, Priscilla. *AMC's Best Day Hikes in New Jersey: Four-Season Guide to 50 of the Best Trails in the Garden State, from the Skylands to the Shore*. Boston: Appalachian Mountain Club Books, 2019.

Geary, Rick. *Lovers' Lane: The Hall-Mills Mystery*. New York: ComicsLit, 2012.

Genovese, Peter. *New Jersey Curiosities: Quirky Characters, Roadside Oddities and Other Offbeat Stuff*. 3rd ed. Guilford, CT: Globe Pequot, 2011.

Gillespie, Angus Kress, and Michael Aaron Rockland. *Looking for America on the New Jersey Turnpike*. New Brunswick, NJ: Rutgers University Press, 1989.

McCloy, James F., and Ray Miller Jr. *The Jersey Devil*. Wilmington, DE: Middle Atlantic, 1976.

McPhee, John. *The Pine Barrens*. New York: Farrar, Straus and Giroux, 1967.

Mulvihill, Andy, and Jake Rossen. *Action Park: Fast Times, Wild Rides, and the Untold Story of America's Most Dangerous Amusement Park*. New York: Penguin Books, 2020.

Regal, Brian, and Frank J. Esposito. *The Secret History of the Jersey Devil: How Quakers, Hucksters, and Benjamin Franklin Created a Monster*. Baltimore: Johns Hopkins University Press, 2018.

Reyn, Irina, ed. *Living on the Edge of the World: New Jersey Writers Take On the Garden State*. New York: Touchstone, 2007.

Sceurman, Mark, and Mark Moran. *Weird N.J.: Your Travel Guide to New Jersey's Local Legends and Best Kept Secrets*. New York: Barnes and Noble, 2003.

Spehr, Paul C. *The Movies Begin: Making Movies in New Jersey, 1887–1920*. Newark, NJ: Newark Museum, 1977.

Tresniowski, Alex. *The Rope: A True Story of Murder, Heroism, and the Dawn of the NAACP*. New York: Simon and Schuster, 2021.

Vallese, Joe, and Alicia A. Beale, eds. *What's Your Exit? A Literary Detour through New Jersey*. Middletown, NJ: Word Riot, 2010.

About the Contributors

Lauren H. Adams is a documentary and landscape photographer from southern New Jersey. She received her BFA in photography from University of the Arts in Philadelphia. Since returning to New Jersey after nearly a decade in Philadelphia, she has encountered and documented hundreds of discarded sofas throughout her daily travels.

Kamelia Ani is a writer, journalism student, and photographer who focuses on street portraits, weddings, and motorcycle racing. She has written for publications including the *Tri City News*, *The Relay*, and the *Brookdale Current*. She lives in Tinton Falls, New Jersey. Her work can be found at kameliaani.com.

Linda J. Barth has written two books on the D&R Canal and three children's books, in addition to *A History of Inventing in New Jersey* and *New Jersey Originals*. She taught in the Bridgewater-Raritan School District for twenty-five years. She is the director of the League of Historical Societies and president of the D&R Canal Watch.

Miko Beach is a transgender creative based in Atlantic City, New Jersey. Beach has explored street photography and video production and now uses imagery as a marketing tool for his merchandise. He enjoys designing his own graphic art and getting his hands messy with paint.

Alexandra Beguez is an illustrator and cartoonist who weaves together images, text, and a bit of whimsy to explore complex ideas. Her work has appeared in *The Nib*, *The Believer Magazine*, and *Guantanamo Voices*, among others. She has been recognized by the Society of Illustrators, *3x3*, *Creative Quarterly*, and *Latin American Ilustración*.

Julie Benbassat is an illustrator whose work combines inspiration from the natural world, old etchings, and life sketching. Her work has been featured in the *New York Times*, PLANSPONSOR, and Workman Publishing.

Kasey Bohnert was born and raised in New Jersey and spends most of her time as a packaging designer. She can be found traveling, printmaking, or roaming around the flower district in New York City. More of her work can be found at kaseybohnert.com.

Caiti Borruso is a photographer and writer from Cliffwood Beach, New Jersey, currently based in San Diego.

Kristen Broderick is a web and graphic designer based in Asbury Park, New Jersey. Away from her computer, she enjoys spending time at the beach and in all places that make New Jersey special! Find her at kristenbroderick.com.

Veronica Casson is a Portland-based comic book illustrator, storyboard artist, and graphic designer. Casson has shown in galleries in San Francisco, San Jose, Pacifica, New York City, and San Miguel de Allende, Mexico. She has designed for Viz Media, Tokypop, and others. She created the webcomic *Grind Like a Girl*. She publishes a new comic page every week on Instagram @saltandfog.

Erica Commisso completed her graduate degree in journalism at NYU and lived in Hoboken while completing her studies. She's a lifelong hockey fan and a freelance writer.

Jonathan Conner (LANK) is an artist, educator, and avid bicycle rider from Trenton, New Jersey. LANK has shown work in galleries around the world and participated in public art and mural projects throughout New Jersey.

Alicia Cook is a best-selling, award-winning poet and essayist. Cook dedicates much of her life to shedding light on how drug addiction impacts the mental health of families. Her latest poetry collection is *Sorry I Haven't Texted You Back*.

Brittany Coppla is a writer from New Jersey, now living in Chicago. She holds an MFA in creative writing from Sarah Lawrence College and has been published in *Adroit*, *Carve Magazine*, *Barren Magazine*, and more. Her work is inspired by food, memory, and the people and places she calls home.

Mike Dawson is the author of *The Fifth Quarter* series and several other graphic novels. His work has been nominated for multiple Eisner and Ignatz Awards, as well as the Slate Cartoonists Studio Prize. He lives at the Jersey Shore with his wife and children.

Carlos Dengler is an actor, musician, writer, and filmmaker living in New York City. He has written for *n+1* and Seven Stories Press and is working on a memoir. In 2016, he performed a critically acclaimed one-person show for the New York International Fringe Festival and guest performed with the *Late Night with Seth Meyers* house band. He has an MFA from NYU Grad Acting. Carlos was the founding bass player and keyboardist for the band Interpol from 1997 to 2010.

Lisa Rosalie Eisenberg is a cartoonist and educator who lives and works in Portland, Oregon. Her comics have appeared in *The Nib* and *The Lily*. She is the author of the graphic novel *We Should Meet in Air*—a story that is part memoir, part Sylvia Plath autobiography.

Alex Flannery is a designer, illustrator, and screen printer based in northern New Jersey, who can often be found at a New Jersey Devils game or binge-watching *The X-Files*. See his work at alexflannery.com.

Stacey Mei Yan Fong was born in Singapore and raised in Hong Kong. She attended college in Savannah, Georgia, and currently resides in Brooklyn, New York, where everything in her apartment is covered in a light dusting of flour. Her cookbook, *50 Pies, 50 States*, is due out on the Fourth of July 2023.

Michael C. Gabriele is a New Jersey author who has written four books on Garden State history. A 1975 graduate of Montclair State University, he has been a journalist and freelance writer for over forty years.

Chris Gethard is a comedian, actor, author, and podcaster raised in West Orange, NJ.

Hassan Ghanny is a writer and performer based in Boston, Massachusetts. Originally from Passaic, he can still tell you the best places to get comida criolla in the 973. His written work has been featured in the *Boston Globe* and on the website of WBUR.

Lorraine Goodman has a BA from Princeton and a master's from NYU/Stern. She has performed on Broadway. She runs the Trenton-based nonprofit Latin American Legal Defense and Education Fund and spends her weekends developing her cruciverbalist skills.

Brandon Harrison is a creative who has produced written, audio, and visual content for a variety of outlets. He curates films at a number of international film festivals and was born in Newark, New Jersey. Visit him at brandonaharrison.com.

Frankie Huang is a Chinese American writer and illustrator who focuses on telling diaspora stories. She is, among other things, a proud Rutgers alumna and Jersey girl.

Brittney Ingersoll is a historian and the curator of the Cumberland County Historical Society in Greenwich, New Jersey. She received her master's in American history with a certificate in public history from Rutgers University—Camden. Ingersoll's historical interests are nineteenth-century gender, sexuality, material culture, and social and cultural history.

Tim Kauger is a photographer, filmmaker, and sporadic writer based in the Northeast. He specializes in landscape, automotive, and architectural media. He can be found outdoors almost every day, hiking or exploring interesting places.

Wills Kinsley is president of the Trenton Cycling Revolution and leader of the Social Ride and can usually be seen welding bicycle art live or playing bike polo on Sundays. He is a founding member of Sage Coalition and Gallery 219, fabricator at Z Signs, and ramp builder for Freedom Skatepark.

Mikhaila Leid is an illustrator and cartoonist based in Jersey. They have previously worked for Lush Cosmetics, Medium, and more.

Caren Lissner's first novel, *Carrie Pilby*, was made into an independent comedy film streaming on Netflix. She's published essays, investigative pieces, and satire in the *Washington Post*, *The Atlantic*, and the *New York Times*. She grew up in Freehold and Old Bridge. She's working on a new novel. Find her at carenlissner.com.

Pooja Makhijani is the editor of *Under Her Skin: How Girls Experience Race in America* and the author of *Mama's Saris*. Her bylines have appeared in the *New York Times*, the *Village Voice*, the *Washington Post*, NPR, *Real Simple*, *The Atlantic*, *The Cut*, *Teen Vogue*, *VICE*, *Bon Appétit*, *Saveur*, *BuzzFeed*, and more. She had a Notable essay in *The Best American Food Writing 2019*. Visit her at poojamakhijani.com.

Donnie Martino is a writer and director of after-school programming in New York City. His writing has appeared in *As Told by Things'* and *X Marks the Spot*. You can find him on Twitter @dmisunbreakable. His favorite Jersey girl is Luseal from Jenkinson's Aquarium.

Jen A. Miller is the author of *Running: A Love Story* and a regular contributor to the *New York Times*. She lives in Audubon, New Jersey, with her dog, Annie.

Raakhee Mirchandani is a Hoboken-based writer, author, and mother. She is amped to be raising a second-generation Jersey girl, her seven-year-old daughter Satya, who shows great promise of carrying forth the title with guts, grit, and glory.

Dan Misdea is a cartoonist from the great state of New Jersey. His work has appeared in *The New Yorker*, *Air Mail*, *The Weekly Humorist*, and elsewhere. His first picture book, *The Light Inside*, is scheduled for release in 2023.

R Justin McNeill is a South Jersey photographer who specializes in colorful and energetic drone photography. He is an FAA-certified drone operator and has worked in law enforcement for over twenty years. His work, which has been featured on local and network news outlets, provides a unique perspective that only aerial photography can offer.

Kate Morgan is a journalist who writes mostly about science, adventure, and food. She was raised in South Jersey and knows exactly how to navigate a traffic circle.

Donovan Myers is a hobbyist photographer who lives in Egg Harbor Township. Originally born in New Hampshire, he has lived in South Jersey since he was four years old. He has been photographing for a decade, with a recent special interest in photographing all the lighthouses in the US. So far he has captured 260 unique lighthouses.

Scott Neumyer is a writer from Central New Jersey whose work has been published by the *New York Times*, the *Washington Post*, *Rolling Stone*, the *Wall Street Journal*, ESPN, *GQ*, *Esquire*, *Parade*, and more publications. Follow him on Instagram and Twitter @scottneumyer, and find more of his work at scottwrites.com.

Kae Lani Palmisano is the Emmy Award–winning host of WHYY's *Check, Please! Philly*, a television show that explores dining throughout the Philadelphia region. She is the host and writer of WHYY's *Delishtory*, a digital series on the history of food. Her work has appeared in *USA Today*, *KitchenAid Stories*, and elsewhere.

Sarah Prager is a Massachusetts-based writer and speaker who is passionate about everything that has to do with LGBTQ+ history. Visit her at sarahprager.com.

Katie Reynolds is a New Jersey–based photographer and art educator whose work embraces the surreal, utilizing double exposures, psychedelic filters, and natural lighting. Katie loves revisiting places that brought her joy as a child and using experimental techniques to capture the feeling of each place on film. Visit her at katiereyphotography.com and on Instagram @katiereyphotography.

Sean Rynkewicz is a freelance illustrator hailing proudly from Trenton, New Jersey. You can find Rynkewicz online at seanrynkewicz.com and on Instagram @red_sean.

Elise Sacco is a hobby doodler and wildlife enthusiast born and raised in Freehold, NJ.

Erinn Salge is a writer and librarian, originally from Metuchen, who now lives and works in northern New Jersey with her family.

Dan Schenker is best known for being one of over eight million people who live in New Jersey. He is a strategist and photographer, husband to Caity, and dad to Charlotte and Calvin.

Kat Schneider is an illustrator and comics artist currently livin', workin', and daydreamin' in New Jersey with her cat, Lou. She has contributed work to the *New York Times*, the *Washington Post*, and others.

Brian Scully's photography ranges in subject from landscape, portrait, wildlife, drone, and abandoned architecture and has been published online and in print. Brian studied fine art/illustration at William Paterson University and is inspired by impressionism. He lives with his fiancée, two cats, and dog in the North Highlands of New Jersey.

Haley Simone is a music illustrator from the Jersey Shore. Her work revolves around music, often including gig posters, merchandise, and her specialty, live performance drawing. To see more of her work, check out www.haleydrawsmusic.com.

Jacquinn Sinclair is a Boston-based writer. Though she now resides in a city best known for clam chowder and Fenway Park, she's still a Jersey girl at heart. Sinclair has fond memories of spending part of her childhood in southern New Jersey devouring panzarottis and going to diners with her dad. She's a contributing performing arts writer and critic for *WBUR The ARTery*, and her work has appeared in *Boston Art Review*, the *Philadelphia Tribune*, and *Boston.com*.

Christopher Smith is a New Jersey–based entertainment, news, and wedding photographer. Educated in marine science, Smith chose instead to pursue his passion for photography and has since been published in dozens of magazines and newspapers worldwide.

Jaclyn "Jackii" Sovern is a New Jersey–based photographer and drone operator with a BFA in photography from the School of Visual Arts. In 2016, she started Socially Relevantt LLC, a full-service digital agency offering content creation, photography, and day-to-day social media services.

lucy dean stockton lives between New York City (Lenape homeland) and western Massachusetts (Pocumtuc homeland); she works as a farmer, writer, and dilettante.

Brandon Stosuy is cofounder of *The Creative Independent*, cofounder of the Basilica Soundscape festival, and cofounder of Zone 6 Artist Management. He is the author of two children's books (*Music Is*, *We Are Music*) and a three-volume journal and memoir series for Abrams Books (*Make Time for Creativity*, *Stay Inspired*, *Fail Successfully*).

Matthew Taub is a writer whose work has appeared in *Time*, *The Atlantic*, *Atlas Obscura*, and many other publications. Much more importantly, he is a fourth-generation New Jerseyan.

Whit Taylor is an Ignatz Award–winning cartoonist and comics editor. Her work has been published by the *New Yorker*, *Washington Post*, *The*

Nib, and others. She is from Madison but now lives in Maplewood with her husband, baby, and two cats.

Team 1:1 New Jersey is a large community that is re-creating the state of New Jersey in the video game Minecraft through the use of sources like Google Earth and Google Street View.

Emily Thompson is a nationally recognized, award-winning artist who attended the prestigious High School of Art & Design and earned a BFA from the School of Visual Arts. Emily's paintings document the ordinary, the everyday, the disappearing, the nostalgic, the abandoned, and the identity of the American landscape.

Bob Varettoni is a public-relations professional who has spent most of his career in New York and all of his life in New Jersey.

Joy Velasco is an illustrator and proud Central Jerseyan. Using her personal lived experience, she creates works that resonate about relationships, the self, and beauty of the everyday in a whimsical way.

Kate Watt's photography inspiration stems from growing up at the shore. As Watt dives deeper into drone photography, it's like she is seeing her home for the first time, with a new set of eyes.

Tori Wehringer is an aspiring artist residing at the Jersey Shore. New Jersey born and raised, Wehringer has a love for hole-in-the-wall eateries, the boardwalk, and a good cup of coffee. Find her on Facebook at Tori Anne Artworks.

Hallel Yadin is the archives associate at the YIVO Institute for Jewish Research in New York City. She is currently a (remote) MLIS student at the University of Missouri, and she holds a degree in history from Rutgers University. You can find more of her work at hallel.fyi.

About the Editor

Kerri Sullivan is the founder of Jersey Collective (@jerseycollective), one of New Jersey's most popular Instagram accounts. The project has over thirty thousand followers and has received press from *New Jersey Monthly*, the *Asbury Park Press*, News 12 New Jersey, and CBS Philly. Her writing has appeared in *McSweeney's Internet Tendency*, *Podcast Review* (a channel of the *Los Angeles Review of Books*), *The Billfold*, and elsewhere. Sullivan is from Monmouth County but currently lives in North Jersey. You can find her at kerrisullivan.com and on Instagram @ksulphoto.